e.guides

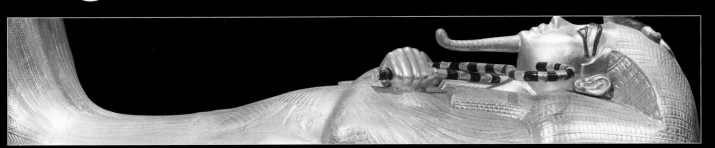

Mummy

London, New York, Melbourne,
Munich and Delhi

Author Peter Chrisp

Project Editors Simon Holland, Patricia Moss, Selina Wood

Weblink Editors Clare Lister, Mariza O'Keeffe, John Bennett

Managing Editor Camilla Hallinan

Digital Development Manager Fergus Day
Production Erica Rosen
DTP Coordinator Toby Beedell
DTP Designer Tony Cutting

Category Publisher Sue Grabham

Consultant Joyce Filer

Project Designers Sarah Cowley, Spencer Holbrook,
Adrienne Hutchinson, Sara Nunan, Johnny Pau, Claire Watson
Cartography Simon Mumford

Managing Art Editor Sophia M. Tampakopoulos Turner

Picture Research Michèle Faram
Picture Librarian Sarah Mills

Jacket Neal Cobourne

Art Director Simon Webb

First American Edition, 2004

Published in the United States by DK Publishing, Inc.,
375 Hudson Street, New York, New York 10014

04 05 06 07 08 10 9 8 7 6 5 4 3 2 1

Published in Great Britain by Dorling Kindersley Limited.

Library of Congress Cataloging-in-Publication Data

Chrisp, Peter
    Mummy / written by Peter Chrisp. -- 1st American ed.
        p. cm. -- (DK Google e.guides)
    Includes index.
    ISBN 0-7566-0760-4
    1. Mummies. 2. Ice mummies. 3. Embalming. I. Title. II. Series.
    GN293.C56 2004
    393' .3--dc22

                                        2004005203

Color reproduction by Media Development and Printing, UK
Printed in China by Toppan Printing Co. (Shenzen) Ltd.

Discover more at
www.dk.com

e.guides

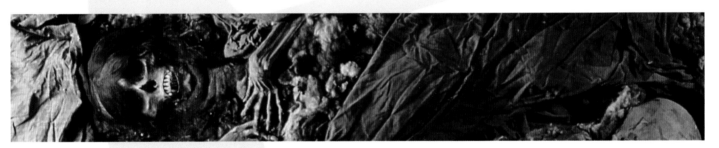

Mummy

Written by **Peter Chrisp**

Google

CONTENTS

How to use the e.guides Web site

e.guides Mummy has its own Web site, created by DK and Google™. When you look up a subject in the book, the article gives you key facts and displays a keyword that links you to extra information online. Just follow these easy steps.

http://www.mummy.dke-guides.com

 Enter this Web site address...

Address : http://www.mummy.dke-guides.com

 Find the keyword in the book...

 Enter the keyword...

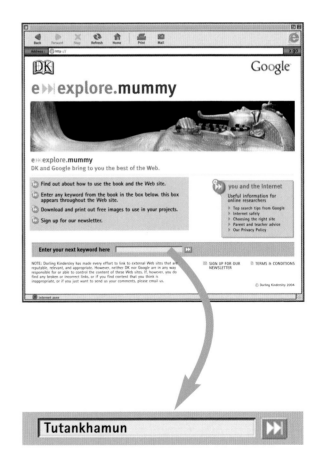

You can only use the keywords from the book to search on our Web site for the specially selected DK/Google links.

Be safe while you are online:

- Always get permission from an adult before connecting to the Internet.

- Never give out personal information about yourself.

- Never arrange to meet someone you have talked to online.

- If a site asks you to log in with your name or email address, ask permission from an adult first.

- Do not reply to emails from strangers—tell an adult.

Parents: Dorling Kindersley actively and regularly reviews and updates the links. However, content may change. Dorling Kindersley is not responsible for any site but its own. We recommend that children are supervised while online, that they do not use chat rooms, and that filtering software is used to block unsuitable material.

Click on your chosen link...

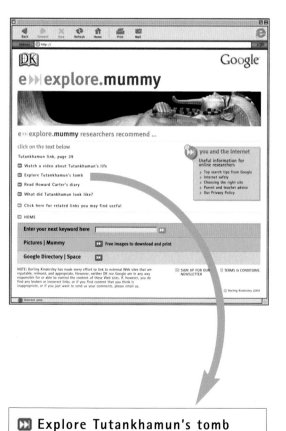

▶▶ **Explore Tutankhamun's tomb**

Links include animations, videos, sound buttons, virtual tours, interactive quizzes, databases, timelines, and real-time reports.

Download fantastic pictures...

Pictures | Mummy ▶▶

Wadjet eye

The pictures are free of charge, but can be used for personal, noncommercial use only.

Go back to the book for your next subject...

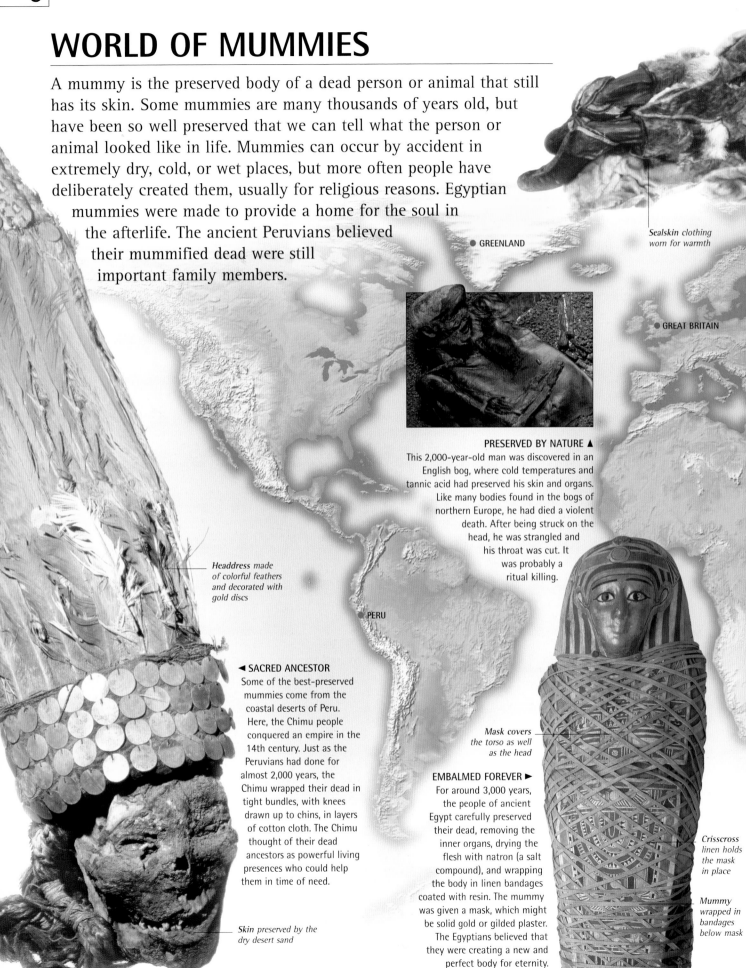

WORLD OF MUMMIES

A mummy is the preserved body of a dead person or animal that still has its skin. Some mummies are many thousands of years old, but have been so well preserved that we can tell what the person or animal looked like in life. Mummies can occur by accident in extremely dry, cold, or wet places, but more often people have deliberately created them, usually for religious reasons. Egyptian mummies were made to provide a home for the soul in the afterlife. The ancient Peruvians believed their mummified dead were still important family members.

GREENLAND

Sealskin clothing worn for warmth

GREAT BRITAIN

PRESERVED BY NATURE ▲
This 2,000-year-old man was discovered in an English bog, where cold temperatures and tannic acid had preserved his skin and organs. Like many bodies found in the bogs of northern Europe, he had died a violent death. After being struck on the head, he was strangled and his throat was cut. It was probably a ritual killing.

Headdress made of colorful feathers and decorated with gold discs

PERU

◄ SACRED ANCESTOR
Some of the best-preserved mummies come from the coastal deserts of Peru. Here, the Chimu people conquered an empire in the 14th century. Just as the Peruvians had done for almost 2,000 years, the Chimu wrapped their dead in tight bundles, with knees drawn up to chins, in layers of cotton cloth. The Chimu thought of their dead ancestors as powerful living presences who could help them in time of need.

Skin preserved by the dry desert sand

Mask covers the torso as well as the head

EMBALMED FOREVER ►
For around 3,000 years, the people of ancient Egypt carefully preserved their dead, removing the inner organs, drying the flesh with natron (a salt compound), and wrapping the body in linen bandages coated with resin. The mummy was given a mask, which might be solid gold or gilded plaster. The Egyptians believed that they were creating a new and perfect body for eternity.

Crisscross linen holds the mask in place

Mummy wrapped in bandages below mask

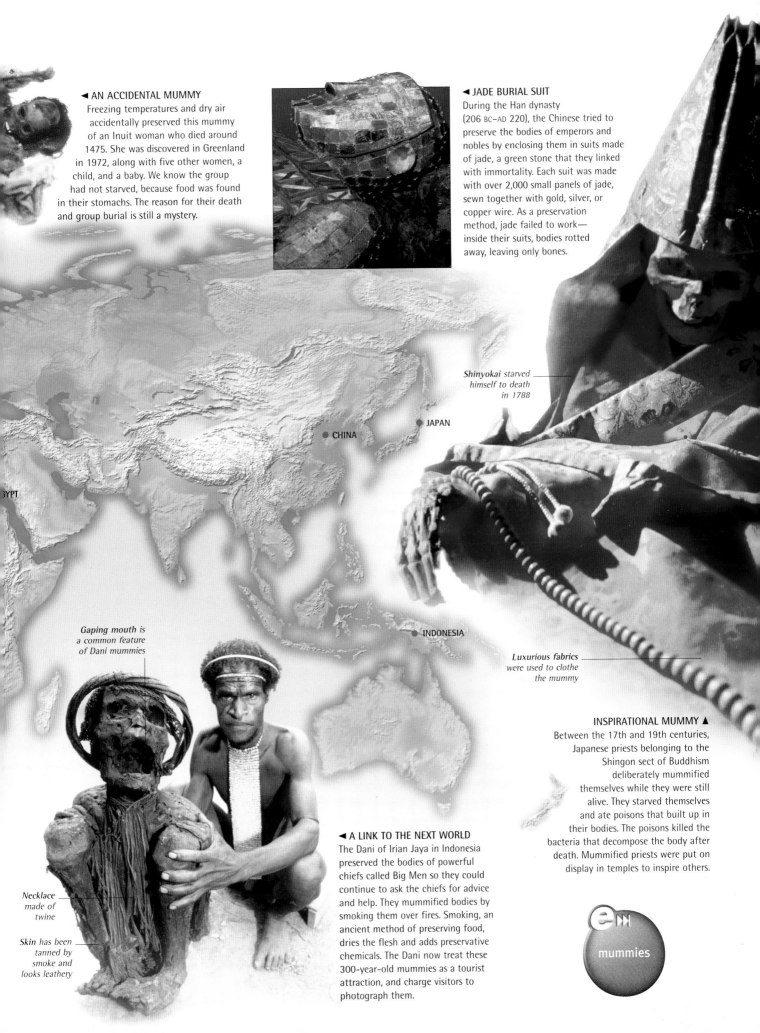

◄ AN ACCIDENTAL MUMMY
Freezing temperatures and dry air accidentally preserved this mummy of an Inuit woman who died around 1475. She was discovered in Greenland in 1972, along with five other women, a child, and a baby. We know the group had not starved, because food was found in their stomachs. The reason for their death and group burial is still a mystery.

◄ JADE BURIAL SUIT
During the Han dynasty (206 BC–AD 220), the Chinese tried to preserve the bodies of emperors and nobles by enclosing them in suits made of jade, a green stone that they linked with immortality. Each suit was made with over 2,000 small panels of jade, sewn together with gold, silver, or copper wire. As a preservation method, jade failed to work— inside their suits, bodies rotted away, leaving only bones.

Shinyokai starved himself to death in 1788

GYPT

● CHINA   ● JAPAN

● INDONESIA

Luxurious fabrics were used to clothe the mummy

Gaping mouth is a common feature of Dani mummies

Necklace made of twine

Skin has been tanned by smoke and looks leathery

◄ A LINK TO THE NEXT WORLD
The Dani of Irian Jaya in Indonesia preserved the bodies of powerful chiefs called Big Men so they could continue to ask the chiefs for advice and help. They mummified bodies by smoking them over fires. Smoking, an ancient method of preserving food, dries the flesh and adds preservative chemicals. The Dani now treat these 300-year-old mummies as a tourist attraction, and charge visitors to photograph them.

INSPIRATIONAL MUMMY ▲
Between the 17th and 19th centuries, Japanese priests belonging to the Shingon sect of Buddhism deliberately mummified themselves while they were still alive. They starved themselves and ate poisons that built up in their bodies. The poisons killed the bacteria that decompose the body after death. Mummified priests were put on display in temples to inspire others.

mummies

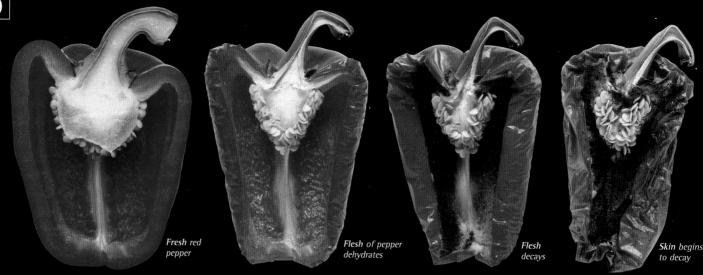

Fresh red pepper

Flesh of pepper dehydrates

Flesh decays

Skin begins to decay

THE SCIENCE OF DECAY

After death, bodies generally begin to decompose very quickly. Our intestines are full of bacteria, which are usually kept under control by the immune system. When we die, the bacteria are free to eat their host body. Flies are attracted to the corpse and lay eggs around bodily openings. These hatch into maggots, which move into the body and start to consume it. As the corpse decays, it releases gases, which attract more flies and other insects. It can take as little as ten days for a corpse to be reduced to bones. Only in special circumstances can bodily decay be prevented.

▲ DECAYING RED PEPPER

Animals and plants are made up of billions of minute cells. Each cell, covered by a thin membrane, contains water and enzymes—proteins that the cell uses to process nutrients. Death occurs when the cells no longer function. After death, the enzymes break down the cell membranes, releasing the water. It is the loss of water that causes this red pepper to shrivel up.

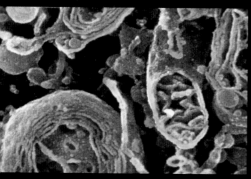

▲ DIGESTIVE ENZYMES

After someone dies, food-digesting bacteria in their intestines begin to feed on the intestines and surrounding organs. Lysosomes, shown above, are tiny membranes in intestinal cells that squirt digestive enzymes onto food. After death, the enzymes escape the lysosomes, destroy the surrounding cell, and spread out. This speeds up the decomposition of the body.

Feet are completely dried out

Tattoo on the skin of the temple is still preserved

◄ SALTED BODY

The organisms that cause decay require warmth, oxygen, and moisture to live. If any of these conditions are missing, a body can be preserved naturally. In about 1000 BC, this man was buried in the Takla Makan Desert of China. He was probably buried during the winter, when freezing temperatures would have killed off any bacteria. High levels of salt in the soil then dried out his body to create this natural mummy.

UNEXPLAINED MUMMY ▲

Sometimes, bodies can be preserved for unknown reasons. These are the feet of Saint Francis Xavier, who was buried on an island off China in 1552. Although his body was said to be covered with quicklime, which speeds up decomposition, it was later dug up and found to be perfectly preserved. It is possible that there were certain chemicals in the soil that are hostile to bacteria. To Catholics, his preservation is a miracle—a sign of his holiness.

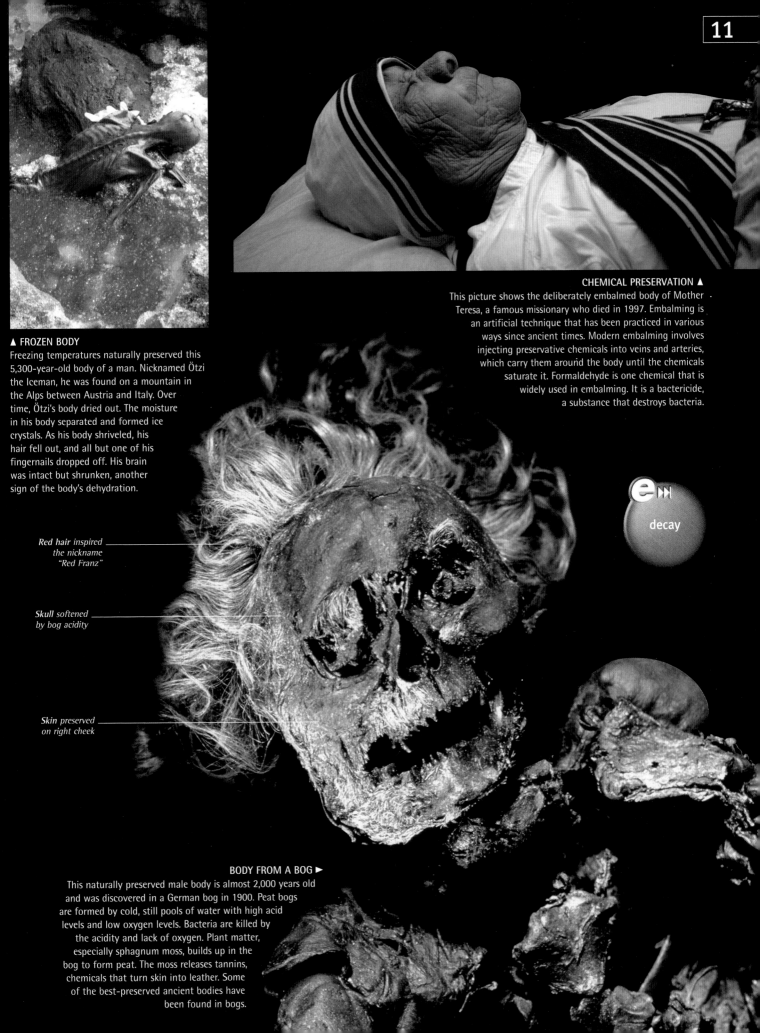

▲ FROZEN BODY

Freezing temperatures naturally preserved this 5,300-year-old body of a man. Nicknamed Ötzi the Iceman, he was found on a mountain in the Alps between Austria and Italy. Over time, Ötzi's body dried out. The moisture in his body separated and formed ice crystals. As his body shriveled, his hair fell out, and all but one of his fingernails dropped off. His brain was intact but shrunken, another sign of the body's dehydration.

CHEMICAL PRESERVATION ▲

This picture shows the deliberately embalmed body of Mother Teresa, a famous missionary who died in 1997. Embalming is an artificial technique that has been practiced in various ways since ancient times. Modern embalming involves injecting preservative chemicals into veins and arteries, which carry them around the body until the chemicals saturate it. Formaldehyde is one chemical that is widely used in embalming. It is a bactericide, a substance that destroys bacteria.

Red hair inspired the nickname "Red Franz"

Skull softened by bog acidity

Skin preserved on right cheek

decay

BODY FROM A BOG ▶

This naturally preserved male body is almost 2,000 years old and was discovered in a German bog in 1900. Peat bogs are formed by cold, still pools of water with high acid levels and low oxygen levels. Bacteria are killed by the acidity and lack of oxygen. Plant matter, especially sphagnum moss, builds up in the bog to form peat. The moss releases tannins, chemicals that turn skin into leather. Some of the best-preserved ancient bodies have been found in bogs.

ANCIENT EGYPT

Five thousand years ago, the Egyptians created one of the world's first and most impressive civilizations. They invented writing, devised a calendar, and built enormous stone temples and tombs. Their civilization lasted, with remarkably few changes, for around 3,000 years. One reason for this was that Egypt was protected from foreign invaders and influence by wide stretches of desert. The Egyptians believed they lived in a perfect world, overseen by gods, and ruled by the gods' living representative, the pharaoh.

ANCIENT EGYPT

Mediterranean Sea

ALEXANDRIA
Lower Egypt CAIRO *(modern capital)*
GIZA
MEMPHIS
SAQQARA

Upper Egypt ABYDOS
VALLEY OF THEBES
THE KINGS *(Luxor)*
EDFU
ASWAN
(modern city)

ABU SIMBEL

N

MUMMY PERIOD: c. 3200 BC–c. AD 392

OLDEST MUMMY: found at Saqqara in 2003

PHARAOH GOD ▶
An Egyptian pharaoh was much more than a king; he was thought of as a living god. Rameses II (who reigned from around 1279 to 1213 BC), for example, was revered as the living embodiment of the sky god Horus. When he died and was mummified, he became united with Horus's father, Osiris, who was ruler of the dead. The Egyptians believed it was thanks to the religious rituals performed by Rameses II that life in Egypt continued—the pharaoh helped make the Nile flood and the crops grow in the fields.

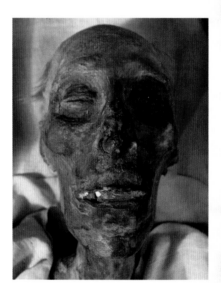

TEMPLE OF RAMESES ▶
At Abu Simbel to the south of Egypt, in Nubia (now called Sudan), Rameses built a great temple to impress the Nubians. Carved out of solid rock, its hall is lined with colossal statues of the pharaoh, who was worshiped here alongside three other gods: Ptah, the creator, Amun, king of the gods, and Re (or Ra), the sun god. Statues of Rameses and the gods sit in the dark shrine at the rear of the temple.

◀ LAND OF THE NILE
Egyptian civilization depended on the Nile River, which cuts through the north African desert. Every year, as snow in the southern mountains melted, the Nile flooded, bringing fertile silt (fine soil) in its waters. When the water subsided, the silt was left behind on the riverbank, ready for planting crops in. This gave the Egyptians a strong sense that they lived in an ordered world. They knew their river always flowed from the south to the north, and that the sun rose in the east and set in the west.

◀ BUILDING MONUMENTS IN STONE
The Egyptians buried their dead in the western desert, where the sun sank at night. It was here that they built royal tombs, including the world's first large buildings and statues made of stone. This colossal sphinx lies in front of the vast pyramid tomb of Pharaoh Khafra (who lived from around 2558 to 2532 BC), as if on guard. The sphinx has the body of a lion, symbolizing strength, and the face of Khafra himself, representing his royal power.

Ancient
Egypt

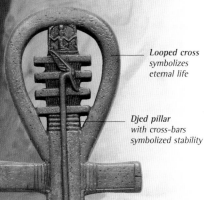

Looped cross
symbolizes
eternal life

Djed pillar
with cross-bars
symbolized stability

Vulture goddess
Nekhbet protected
the pharaoh

Was *scepter* with a forked
base and dog's head was
a symbol of power

▲ THE GIFT OF LIFE

This ankh amulet or charm was found inside the
bandages of a mummy. The ankh was a cross with a
loop on top and symbolized eternal life. In paintings on
temple walls, pharaohs are often shown receiving ankhs
from the gods. The sign was also made into a powerful,
protective amulet worn as a necklace, which the
Egyptians believed had magical powers. Most Egyptians
were illiterate (could not read) and this was one of the
few signs understood by even the poorest people.

Double crown of Upper
and Lower Egypt

Six statues
of Rameses,
30 ft (9 m) high

Door to shrine that
contained statues of
Rameses and the three gods

EGYPTIAN WRITING

The Egyptians invented writing some time
before 3000 BC. There were two basic styles.
Hieroglyphs (holy carvings) were picture
signs used in wall carvings and paintings.
Hieratic (priestly) script was a shorthand
version, invented for writing quickly on
paper made from papyrus.

Hieroglyphs could stand for ideas and
sounds. The owl hieroglyph, on the right,
means in, from, and with. It could also
stand for the sound "m" in other words.

The Egyptians called writing *medu-neter*,
which means "the words of the gods."

HIEROGLYPHS

HIERATIC SCRIPT

EGYPT'S PYRAMIDS

The pyramids of Egypt are the largest and most accurately constructed stone buildings of the ancient world. Each royal pyramid was a tomb for a dead pharaoh. Unlike his palace, built of mud-brick, a pharaoh's pyramid was built of stone because it was intended to last for all eternity. Texts written on the walls of burial chambers suggest that a pyramid was also a kind of launch pad. It was designed to project the soul of the dead pharaoh into the sky, where he would live among the Imperishable Stars forever.

ENTERING THE GREAT PYRAMID ▼
There have always been stories about the glittering treasures buried within the pyramids. The entrances and passages were concealed with enormous stone plugs, but by 1000 BC, every known pyramid had been looted. At Giza, the original entrance to Khufu's pyramid, shown here, is still sealed; visitors enter the pyramid by a lower hole cut by the Arab leader Caliph-Ma'mun in the 9th century.

Limestone facing was stolen for later buildings

Steps represented a stairway that reached to the gods

▲ THE FIRST PYRAMID
Pyramid-building began with a step pyramid built for Pharaoh Djoser between 2630 BC and 2611 BC. It is 197 ft (60 m) high and was the first pyramid and royal tomb made of stone. Before then, pharaohs were buried in mud-brick tombs called mastabas. Djoser's architect, Imhotep, came up with the revolutionary idea of placing six stone mastabas of decreasing size in a stack. This was like a stairway, helping the pharaoh climb up into the sky.

THE ORIENTATION OF PYRAMIDS

THE CONSTELLATIONS
Some historians believe the pyramids were built to align with star constellations, particularly Orion. The Egyptians linked Orion with their god Osiris, king of the dead. This constellation has three bright stars, which are called Orion's belt. The air shaft in the burial chamber of Khufu's pyramid points toward the belt, supporting this theory.

THE PYRAMID COMPLEX AT GIZA
In 1994, Robert Bauval and Adrian Gilbert argued that the pyramids were positioned to match the stars in Orion. In fact only three pyramids can be lined up with the three stars in Orion's belt. Most experts believe the site was chosen for more practical reasons, especially the need for a flat area of bedrock on which to lay the foundations.

▼ THE GREAT PYRAMID OF KHUFU

Around 2550 BC, Pharaoh Khufu (who reigned from 2589 to 2566 BC) built the largest pyramid of all, the Great Pyramid. It stands 481 ft (147 m) high, and is precisely laid out with its sides facing due north, south, east, and west. The sides at the base are over 755 ft (230 m) long, but, amazingly, the difference between the longest and shortest side is only 7⅞ in (20 cm).

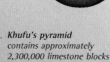

pyramids

The top 33 ft (10 m) have been weathered away

Khufu's pyramid contains approximately 2,300,000 limestone blocks

THE BURIAL CHAMBER ▲

In the heart of his pyramid at Saqqara, Pharaoh Unas (who reigned from 2375 to 2345 BC) lay in a black sarcophagus, the color of fertile soil, ready for rebirth. The burial chamber walls were covered with texts describing his journey to the afterlife. They compare Unas with a leaping grasshopper or a soaring falcon traveling up into the sky. There are also magical spells on the walls designed to protect him on his journey.

INSIDE THE GREAT PYRAMID

Khufu changed his mind about the internal layout of his pyramid several times. There are passages leading to three chambers, each originally intended to house the pharaoh's sarcophagus. Narrow air shafts rise from the upper two chambers toward the surface. Early explorers called the second unfinished chamber the Queen's Chamber, but this room has nothing to do with any queen.

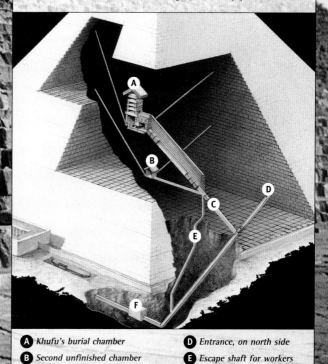

A Khufu's burial chamber

B Second unfinished chamber

C Grand Gallery

D Entrance, on north side

E Escape shaft for workers

F First unfinished chamber

THE MUMMY GODS

According to Egyptian legend, the god Osiris had triumphed over death, and every Egyptian wanted to follow his example. In the legend, Osiris was a good ruler who was murdered by his evil brother Seth. Seth chopped his body into 14 pieces and scattered them along the Nile. Isis, Osiris's widow, carefully searched for the body parts and, with Anubis, god of mummification, put the body back together. This was the very first mummy. Using magic, Isis and Anubis revived Osiris, who became the eternal king of the land of the dead.

◀ JOINING OSIRIS IN THE AFTERLIFE
Osiris, shown here carved on a column at the temple of Horus, Sobek, and Hathor at Kom Ombo, judged the souls of dead people before they entered his kingdom. From an early period, the Egyptians believed their kings joined Osiris in the afterlife, so they prepared their mummies in exactly the same way as the body of Osiris had been long ago. By the later periods, they believed everyone could achieve everlasting life with Osiris, and all Egyptians were mummified.

Egyptian gods

SETH, GOD OF STORMS AND CHAOS ▶
Seth, the killer of Osiris, was the god of storms and chaos. He was the patron of the desert and foreign lands—both regarded as hostile places by Egyptians. Seth was shown with the body of a human and the head of an animal with squared ears and a curved snout, perhaps an aardvark or anteater. This is known as the Typhonian animal, after Seth's later identification with a Greek mythical monster called Typhon.

Horus depicted with a falcon's head and human body

Seth holds a was scepter, which was a symbol of power

◀ HORUS THE SKY GOD
Known as the sky god, Horus was the son of Osiris and Isis. This statuette shows Isis nursing Horus when he was a baby. When he grew up, Horus avenged his father's death by killing Seth and casting him out of Egypt to live in the desert. After his victory over Seth, Horus replaced him as ruler of Egypt. From then on, Horus was the god of kingship as well as the sky. Every pharaoh was thought to be the embodiment of the god, and was called the Living Horus.

◀ KING OF THE UNDERWORLD

In this painting from the Book of the Dead, Osiris sits enthroned as ruler of the underworld and judge of the dead. Thoth, the god of writing, stands before him, recording his judgments. Osiris was shown wrapped in bandages, like a mummy, with a black or green face. Both of these colors were linked with new life. Black was the color of the fertile soil of Egypt, and green was the color of the growing vegetation. Osiris holds a flail and a crook, royal regalia, which were also carried by pharaohs.

Pointed ears, like a jackal's

Collar, like a dog's

Black was the color of new life

▲ ANUBIS, GOD OF MUMMIFICATION

The god of mummification and protector of cemeteries was Anubis. He was represented as a black dog or jackal, or as a man with the head of a dog or a jackal. The argument that he was a dog is supported by his collar and the role of dogs as guards. His pointed ears, however, suggest that he was a jackal. He may have appeared in jackal form to prevent real jackals, which were scavengers, from disturbing the dead.

BECOMING IMMORTAL ▶

With the help of the gods, every Egyptian hoped to be made immortal after death. This pectoral (breast ornament), worn by the mummy of Tutankhamun, shows the dead pharaoh's transformation into an immortal. At the centre are two cartouches. The cartouche on the left spells his birth name – Tutankhamun. The one on the right spells his throne name – Nebkheprere. The cartouches are being carried up into the sky by the scarab beetle, Khepri, a god linked with rebirth. The solar disk at the top is Ra (or Re), the sun god, welcoming Tutankhamun to the heavens.

Ra, the sun god, with outstretched, protective wings

Isis holds the beetle's wing

Nephthys, the sister of Isis, holds the beetle's wing

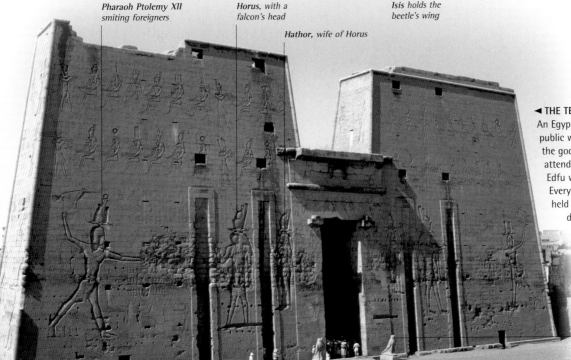

Pharaoh Ptolemy XII smiting foreigners

Horus, with a falcon's head

Hathor, wife of Horus

◀ THE TEMPLE OF HORUS

An Egyptian temple was not a place of public worship. It was thought of as the god's home, where his statue was attended to by priests. This temple at Edfu was the earthly home of Horus. Every December, a great festival was held here. It included a sacred drama, in which the priests reenacted the struggle between Horus and Seth. This is thought to be the world's oldest known play.

Statues of Horus guard the pylon (ceremonial gateway)

THE VIEW OF DEATH

The Egyptians developed a complex view of life and death. Every person was made up of several elements. The most obvious one was the physical body, but equally real and important were a person's name and shadow. There were also two spirit forms, called the *ka* and the *ba*. After death, these two forms were thought to unite in the underworld to form a third spirit being, the *akh*. It was as an *akh* that the dead person lived again in the underworld, which was thought to be a land like Egypt.

◄ THE PRESERVED BODY

The Egyptians thought of death as a temporary stage in our life cycle before becoming immortal and living forever. For this transformation to be successful, the corpse had to be made stable and enduring. This was done by turning it into a mummy, which could be brought back to life by magic. The mummy was thought of as a new and perfect body, which would last for eternity.

1. *Real rings* were placed on the mummy's fingers

2. *Sky goddess Nut* wraps her wings around the mummy

3. *Plaque* showing Anubis, the god of embalming

4. *Shabti* figure to perform tasks in the afterlife

▲ THE SETTING SUN

The dead were believed to live in the west, where the sun disappeared each night, traveling down to the underworld. The reappearance of the sun in the east each morning symbolized renewal and rebirth. Living by the Nile, the Egyptians imagined the sun made its daily and nightly journey on a boat. For them, the sun god, Ra (or Re), was the great creator and the master of life.

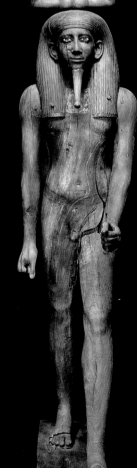

Raised hand shows that this is a ka statue

THE LIFE FORCE ►

The ka was a person's life force, created at his or her birth. After death, it lived in the tomb, known as the house of the ka. It was the *ka* who received most of the offerings given to the dead. Its symbol was two raised hands, sometimes shown on statues of the deceased. The *ka* entered such statues to make them come to life, just as the *ka*s of gods were believed to enter their statues in the temples. This is the *ka* statue of Pharaoh Awibra Hor, dating from around 1700 BC.

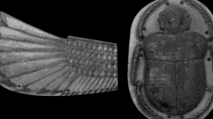

SCARAB

▲ PROTECTING THE HEART

This scarab is a magical amulet, placed over the heart to protect it. For the Egyptians, the heart was the most important part of the body. They believed that intelligence lay in the heart, not in the brain, and that the heart contained a person's moral being: their goodness or wickedness. As a result, the heart was the only organ to be put back into the mummy. After death, in the underworld, the heart was tested, and the hearts of the wicked were devoured.

◄ THE NAME

To an Egyptian, a person's name was an important living part of them. A baby did not truly live until it had been named, and people whose names were forgotten ceased to exist. This was why pharaohs had their names carved on all their monuments, in oval shapes called cartouches. Some pharaohs' names were defaced by their successors, who hoped to destroy them in the afterlife.

Magical rope protects the pharaoh's name

◄ THE SPIRIT

The *ba* was shown as a human-headed bird. This represented a person's ability to move around and be changed into other forms. At night the *ba* remained in the tomb, but each day it flew outside to enjoy the cool breezes. The *ba* also traveled down to the underworld, where it reunited with the *ka* to create the *akh*. It was as an *akh* that the blessed dead inhabited the underworld.

Hieroglyphs spell "Thutmose" for the name of Pharaoh Thutmose III

underworld

Painting of a dead body

WORKERS FOR THE AFTERLIFE

The Egyptians thought of the next world as a land like Egypt, where heavy farm work had to be done. To avoid this work, people were buried with statuettes called shabtis, or "answerers," who would labor on their behalf. Shabtis were covered with magical spells designed to activate them. A typical spell would say, "O shabti, if (name of deceased) be summoned to do any work which is to be done in the realm of the dead—to make the fields fertile, to irrigate the land, or to convey sand from east to west—'Here am I,' you shall say, 'I shall do it.'"

These shabtis, dating from 1250 BC, belonged to Princess Henutmehyt. She is shown on the side of the box worshiping the sons of Horus, the gods who protected the organs of the dead.

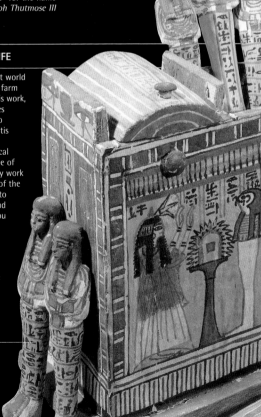

Wooden shabti with magical spells

THE SHADOW ▲

At death, the shadow separated itself from the body, and was able to move around independently, at great speed. Like the *ka*, it was given offerings in tombs and tomb chapels. Prayers were said to protect it from harmful demons, which were believed to devour shadows. Destroying someone's shadow was another way of ending their existence.

THE MUMMY-MAKERS

Egyptian mummification was a complex technical procedure, designed to preserve the body. It was also a set of religious rituals performed by priests, and a magical act intended to recreate exactly the making of the very first mummy of the god Osiris by Anubis. Throughout the 70-day process, spells were recited to make the mummification effective. At the end, one of the priests addressed the mummy, saying, "You will live again, you will live forever. Behold, you are young again forever."

e▸▸
embalming

◀ **MASK OF ANUBIS**
A priest known as the Overseer of Mysteries was in charge of the mummification. He wore the mask of the jackal, or dog, called Anubis, and played his role. He had two assistants, the Lector Priest, who read out the spells, and the Seal Bearer of the God. The priests' assistants oversaw a team of Bandagers, who did the physical work of preparing the body.

◀ **HERODOTUS (484–432 BC)**
The Greek historian and traveler Herodotus visited Egypt in about 450 BC. He interviewed Egyptian priests who explained how they preserved the dead. There were three mummification methods, each costing a different fee. The rich could afford the full treatment, with spices, amulets, bandages, and canopic jars. The bodies of the poor were simply dried with natron and returned, unwrapped, to their families.

① **WASHING THE BODY**
The first act in mummification was washing the body with water and natron. Natron was a salt collected from the shores of Egyptian lakes. It was a type of disinfectant but it also had a ritual purpose, purifying the dead. Then the priest pushed a rod up the nose to punch a hole in the skull. Brain hooks were used to scoop the brain out, which was thrown away. Next, the priest made an incision in the side of the body and removed the organs. The heart was saved and put back later. The intestines, stomach, liver, and lungs were preserved in separate canopic jars

Embalmer pours water from a jug over the body

Body is purified with streams of water

RITUAL FLINT KNIFE

CANOPIC JAR FOR INTESTINES

HOOKS TO REMOVE BRAIN THROUGH NOSE

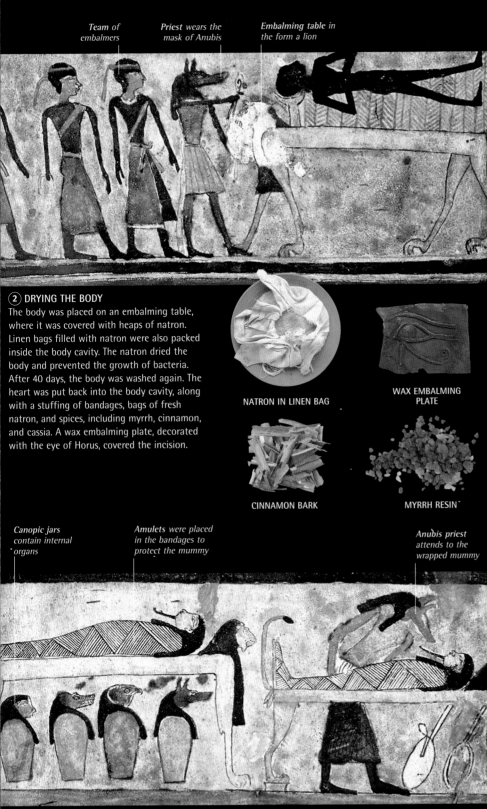

Team of embalmers

Priest wears the mask of Anubis

Embalming table in the form a lion

② DRYING THE BODY

The body was placed on an embalming table, where it was covered with heaps of natron. Linen bags filled with natron were also packed inside the body cavity. The natron dried the body and prevented the growth of bacteria. After 40 days, the body was washed again. The heart was put back into the body cavity, along with a stuffing of bandages, bags of fresh natron, and spices, including myrrh, cinnamon, and cassia. A wax embalming plate, decorated with the eye of Horus, covered the incision.

NATRON IN LINEN BAG

WAX EMBALMING PLATE

CINNAMON BARK

MYRRH RESIN

Canopic jars contain internal organs

Amulets were placed in the bandages to protect the mummy

Anubis priest attends to the wrapped mummy

③ WRAPPING THE BODY

After the body was stuffed, it was coated with resin. Made from the sap of fir or pine trees, the resin protected the skin and also smelled sweet. Over a 15-day period, the body was then wrapped in long linen bandages, with more resin poured on top. The wrappings contained up to 20 alternating layers of shrouds and bandages. Protective amulets were placed within the wrappings, each in a particular position laid down in religious texts.

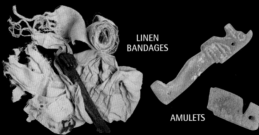

LINEN BANDAGES

AMULETS

▲ COFFIN CASE

This wooden coffin, made around 600 BC for a man called Djedbastiufankh, shows scenes of the mummification process. After the mummy was wrapped, it was given a new face with eyes so that it could see again. This might be a mask tied on to the mummy, or a face carved on a coffin lid, or both. It was then ready for the funeral, when more magic spells would be used to restore it to life.

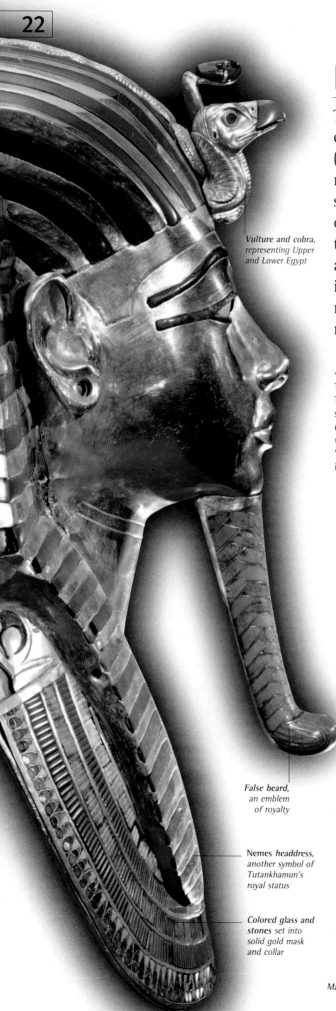

*Vulture and cobra,
representing Upper
and Lower Egypt*

MASKS AND COFFINS

Throughout Egypt's long history, there were many changes in the style of masks, coffins, and sarcophagi (stone coffin containers). Rectangular boxes were replaced by human-shaped ones, which were either single or made up of several coffins that fitted inside one another. The purpose of these objects remained the same. Egyptians saw a coffin or sarcophagus as a magical container to protect the body and ensure its survival in the tomb and afterlife. Like a masked mummy, a human-shaped coffin also acted as a new, substitute body for the dead person.

◄ MAGICAL MASK
This golden mask covered the head and shoulders of Pharaoh Tutankhamun's mummy. To protect the mummy, it has magic spells inscribed on its shoulders and back. They identify the dead king with Osiris, and the different parts of the mask with different gods. The spells addressing the mask say, "Your forehead is that of Anubis, the nape of your neck is that of Horus... You are in front of Osiris."

embalming

*Tutankhamun riding
his chariot*

CLOTHES BOX ►
This painted wooden chest, found in Tutankhamun's tomb, held the pharaoh's clothes and is decorated with scenes of him hunting and fighting battles. Unlike the masks and coffins, this box has a practical rather than a magical function. If the magical spells of the mummy-makers succeeded in bringing the pharaoh back to life, he would need access to his clothes and all his precious belongings.

*False beard,
an emblem
of royalty*

*Nemes headdress,
another symbol of
Tutankhamun's
royal status*

*Colored glass and
stones set into
solid gold mask
and collar*

*Idealized face
of the dead
priestess*

*Arms crossed
in the pose
of Osiris*

*Red straps worn
by the priesthood*

PROTECTED PRIESTESS ►
This is the wooden coffin of a priestess from Thebes who died in around 1000 BC. The beautifully wrapped mummy inside the coffin is not wearing a mask. The carved and painted face on the coffin lid was designed to be the priestess's new face in the afterlife. The protective function of the coffin is shown by the gods painted on the lid. They have outstretched vulture wings, which represented encirclement and protection.

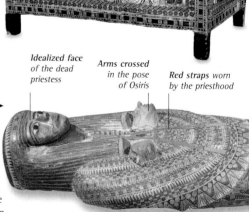

*Large linen shroud covers
wrapped mummy beneath*

*Magic spells, written in hieroglyphs,
cover the lower part of the coffin*

Base *of inner coffin*

Youthful face, *in gold like the sun*

Base *of outer coffin*

Gilded *body mask*

Lid *of inner coffin*

Lid *of outer coffin*

Outer lid *decorated with strips, like a bandaged mummy*

ORGAN PROTECTION

STORAGE BOX

Just as the mummified body needed magical protection, so did the organs that had been removed during mummification. The Egyptians knew they would need these organs in the next life, and hoped to be reunited with them through magic.

The organs were protected by being placed in canopic jars, watched over by four gods. These were the sons of Horus: human-headed Imsety, who cared for the liver; baboon-headed Hapy, who looked after the lungs; jackal-headed Duamutef, who protected the stomach; and hawk-headed Qebhsenuef, who cared for the intestines.

The jars are called canopic after a mistaken belief that they were connected with the Egyptian town of Canopus, where Osiris was worshiped as a human-headed jar.

LIVER LUNGS STOMACH INTESTINES

◄ NESTED COFFINS

A complete body mask covered the mummy of a priestess called Henutmehit, who was then housed inside two nested coffins. The coffin-makers added the youthful, gilded faces in the hope that she would become young again in the next world. Decorated with gold leaf, this set of coffins was a luxury container for the afterlife. Such coffins were also a symbol of status, since only the rich could afford them. Nested coffins also provided extra security for the body, and more magical protection—they had more space for inscribing spells.

Seven winged *gods appear on the lid*

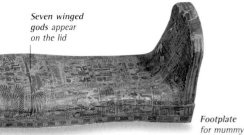

Gods *of the underworld*

Footplate *for mummy to stand on*

Heavy stone lid *offered greater protection from tomb robbers*

STONE SARCOPHAGUS ►

A sarcophagus is a large container for a coffin or mummy. This is the sarcophagus of Ankh-hor, governor of Upper Egypt in the late 7th century BC, and one of the most powerful men in the kingdom. It is made of granite and carved with images of Ankh-hor worshiping the gods. "Sarcophagus" is a Greek word meaning "flesh-eater." The Greeks mistakenly believed that a stone box caused the body inside to decay.

THE FUNERAL

The death of a pharaoh was followed by 70 days of national mourning while his body was mummified. When it was ready for burial, the mummy was placed in a coffin and lifted on to a funeral bier (sled). The bier was hauled by oxen to the bank of the Nile and taken by boat to the western desert. The "westerners," as the dead were called, were buried here, where the sun set. A great funeral procession accompanied the mummy. It included the new pharaoh, priests, and family members. Similar but smaller processions were held at the funerals of ordinary Egyptians.

◄ THE PROCESSION

This funeral procession was painted on a papyrus found in the tomb of a noble called Hunefer. In front of the bier carrying the mummy, the Sem priest is burning incense and scattering milk on the ground to purify the route. Male and female mourners dressed in white escort the bier, which is hauled by oxen. A man carries grave goods to be offered to the gods and for the mummy's use in the afterlife. The men at the rear pull a second bier carrying the canopic jars.

funerals

◄ THE SEM PRIEST

A leading part in the funeral was played by a figure called the Sem priest, identified by the leopard skin he wore. A clue to his function is provided by an inscription from the tomb of Amenemhat addressing the dead: "Your purification is performed by the Sem priest." At the tomb, he scattered water and burned sweet-smelling incense in front of the mummy. During royal funerals, the new pharaoh often took this role.

Sistrum was shaken like a rattle at ceremonial occasions

Loose hair was a sign of mourning

Oars to steer boat

Female mummy shaded by a canopy

Jars containing offerings

Female mourners wore white linen robes

▲ ACROSS THE NILE

Living by the Nile River, it was natural for the Egyptians to think of all long journeys being made by boat. Even for the overland part of the funeral procession, therefore, the mummy was carried on a bier shaped like a boat. Models of boats, like this one from around 1900 to 1850 BC, were placed in the tomb to help the mummy continue on its journey through the underworld.

THE MOURNERS ►

Although the dead were thought to live again, a funeral was still a time of sorrow. Wall paintings in temples show female mourners watching the procession go by. These may have been family members or people hired for the purpose. To show their grief, they tore their clothes, poured ash on their heads, and lifted their arms to the sky, wailing loudly. This ancient custom still continues in Egypt today.

▲ THE OPENING OF THE MOUTH

After the mummy had been placed in the tomb, it was brought back to life with a ritual known as the Opening of the Mouth. The heir of the deceased, or a priest acting on his behalf, would touch the mummy's eyes, ears, nose, and other parts of the body, magically restoring all their functions. Touching the mouth would enable the mummy to talk, eat, and drink.

Forked tool to touch the mummy's face

PRIEST'S TOOLS USED IN THE OPENING OF THE MOUTH

▲ READY FOR FOOD

This wall painting from the tomb of Nebamun shows the dancers and musicians at the funeral banquet, which took place after the Opening of the Mouth ceremony. The mummy, now brought to life in its *ka* form, joined the banquet with the mourners. The lavish banquet, which included wine, meat, fruit, and bread.

Pyramid of Pharaoh Khufu at Giza

THE TOMB ▶

Royal tombs were much grander than those of ordinary Egyptians. They were filled with treasures made of gold and precious stones for the afterlife, so they had to be sealed, like this pyramid at Giza, or concealed in secret locations. Many pharaohs were first entombed in the Valley of the Kings near Luxor, and later moved to secret locations by priests. A pharaoh's offerings were not brought to his tomb, but presented to his statue in a separate mortuary temple.

Tomb of Seshemnufer, a nobleman

INTO THE UNDERWORLD

Before being reborn in the next life, the dead were expected to go on a long and dangerous journey, through a dark underworld inhabited by terrifying monsters. On their journey, they would meet many gods, and also have to pass a test to show that they deserved to live again. Personalized guidebooks for the journey were painted on tomb walls and written on papyrus rolls, which were buried with the dead. These texts, known as *The Chapters of Coming Forth by Day*, listed the dangers that they would encounter, and the magic spells they should recite to protect themselves.

Dead man journeying to the underworld *Khepri, god of rebirth* *Thoth, god of magic and writing*

◄ **MEETING THE GODS**
Thoth, the god of magic and writing, was believed to have written the spells for the underworld journey. He was one of hundreds of gods that the dead would meet. Many of his spells list the names of the underworld gods and monsters, and the proper way of addressing them to win their help or make them harmless. The Egyptians believed that to know someone's name was to have power over them.

Kilt worn by Thoth to show he has a man's body

▲ **BOAT JOURNEY**
Every night, after setting in the west, the sun was believed to travel by boat through the underworld, before being reborn in the eastern sky. The dead took advantage of this by catching a ride on the sun's boat. Here the dead man stands at the back of the boat. Khepri, the scarab god of rebirth and the sun's journey, is in the center. He was thought to roll the sun along, just as a scarab beetle rolls a ball of dung.

▲ **WEIGHING THE HEART**
Anubis, god of mummification, oversaw the key test, which was called the Weighing of the Heart. The heart of the dead person was weighed against a feather of truth. If the heart was lighter than the feather, it meant that the person had lived a good life and he had passed the test to everlastinglife. If the heart was heavy, it meant that the person had led an evil life and he would fail the test. Heavy hearts would be eaten by Ammut, the eater of the dead, who was a mixture of crocodile, lion, and hippopotamus. In fact, Ammut always went hungry, because all the papyri record a successful result.

1 *Dead man, dressed in white, is led toward the scales where his heart will be weighed*

2 *Anubis, holding an ankh or life sign leads the dead man forward*

3 *Balance on the scales is adjusted by Anubis to ensure an accurate reading*

4 *Ammut, the eater of the dead, watches to see if the heart is heavy enough to eat*

5 *Thoth records that the heart is lighter than the feather*

6 *Horus, holding an ankh in his left hand, leads the dead man toward Osiris*

TWO WORLDS ►
The Egyptians thought of the place where the dead lived as a parallel world, where the sun went at night. When the sun sank in one world, it rose in the other. This ceiling painting from the burial chamber of Rameses IX shows the two worlds, separated by two outstretched forms of Nut, the sky goddess. You can see the journey of the sun, a series of red dots, through the body of Nut in the middle of the painting.

underworld

Wife of the dead man — *Dead man stands before Osiris* — *Offerings of food and wine for Osiris* — *Osiris seated on his throne*

▲ MEETING OSIRIS
This papyrus from a nobleman's tomb shows the end of his successful journey to the underworld. He stands before Osiris, his hands raised in adoration. Possession of this papyrus guaranteed that he would be welcomed by Osiris, and so the papyrus functioned as a sort of passport as well as a guidebook. The hieroglyphs on the papyrus tell us that the dead man is demanding to be accepted into Osiris's kingdom.

THE FIELD OF REEDS ►
After their dark journey through the underworld, the dead rose with the sun, and found themselves in a paradise called the Field of Reeds. This kingdom was ruled by Osiris, and was like a perfect version of Egypt. There was no sickness here, and no pests to eat the crops, which grew tall in the fields. The Egyptian afterlife was a wonderful place.

ANIMAL MUMMIES

The most common Egyptian mummies are not of humans but of animals, including cats, dogs, crocodiles, and birds. Some were beloved pets, such as a monkey buried with a princess called Maatkare around 1000 BC. From about 700 BC, animal mummies were made by priests to be sold to worshipers, who left them at temples as gifts to the gods. This was an important source of income for the temples. Such was the demand that animal mummies were sometimes faked. X-rays show that some contain mud, straw, and odd bones rather than the correct animals.

▲ ANCIENT RELATIVES
Crocodiles lived along the edge of the Nile in ancient Egypt, as they do today. The Egyptians feared the crocodiles' ferocity and linked them with Sobek, a god of the Nile. Sobek had the power of a crocodile, and was depicted either as a crocodile or as a man with a crocodile's head. Worshipers who wanted to ask Sobek for help would present him with the mummy of a crocodile, which they bought at one of his temples. The largest mummified crocodile ever found was 15 ft (4.6 m) long.

◄ MUMMIFIED CROCODILES
Crocodiles were mummified in huge numbers at Kom Ombo, where the god Sobek shared a great temple with the god Horus, and at Shedyet, which the Greeks renamed Crocodilopolis ("Crocodile City"). Sobek's temple at Crocodilopolis was like a crocodile zoo, with priests responsible for the breeding, care, and mummification of the sacred beasts. The crocodiles were fed on fine meat and dressed in gold jewelry. Baby crocodiles and eggs were also sold to be offered to the god Sobek.

Feathered atef crown of Osiris on falcon-headed Sokar

ANIMAL GODS ►
Gods could have the features of more than one animal. So Opet, a mother goddess, is shown in this tomb painting from Thebes as a hippo with a crocodile's tail. The figure behind Opet is Hathor, a protective mother-like goddess. Over time, gods also often took on each other's characters and roles. Sokar was a falcon-headed god worshiped in Memphis, where he was seen as the protector of tombs. In time, this led to his identification with Osiris, king of the dead. In this painting he is in the combined form, Osiris-Sokar.

◄ SACRED SHREW
A god could have more than one sacred animal. The goddess Wadjet, for example, was linked with cobras, lions, shrews, and a mongooselike creature called an ichneumon. The ichneumon, active in daytime, represented the goddess during the day. The shrew, which is nocturnal, represented the goddess at night. Shrews were also sacred to the god Horus.

Bronze case for mummified shrew

Linen painted with scales and fins

FISH FOR A GODDESS ▲
Fish were sacred at Mendes, where a fish goddess called Hatmehit was worshiped, and at Oxyrhynchus, a town named after a type of fish. The Oxyrhynchus fish was holy because Egyptians believed it was born from the wounds of Osiris, when his body was scattered in the Nile by Seth. Fish mummies, sometimes of kinds no longer found in the Nile, help create a picture of wildlife in ancient Egypt.

Linen bandage wrapped around neck in the shape of a collar

Gold leaf covers the wooden body

◄ GOLDEN IBIS
The ibis was a bird sacred to Thoth, god of wisdom. Millions of ibis mummies have been found in burial chambers at Saqqara. They were offered not to Thoth but to Imhotep, architect of the first pyramid there. Famed for his wisdom, over time Imhotep had been transformed into a god of healing. The ibises were left by the sick, hoping for a cure, or by people who wished to thank Imhotep for healing them.

Feet and head made of bronze

animal mummies

THE SACRED CAT
Perhaps the most common mummies of all are those of cats, which were bred in vast numbers solely for the purpose of being mummified. So many cats have been found that, in the 19th century, they were shipped abroad to be ground up and made into fertilizer. Cats were sacred to Bastet, a protective mother goddess worshiped at Bubastis. The mummified cat, with the elaborately patterned linen strips, is not what it seems. It contains the head of an adult cat but the body of a four-month-old kitten. It dates from the 2nd or 1st century BC. Most cat mummies contained a complete cat and were wider at the bottom than at the top. Mummies were also placed in cat-shaped coffins made of wood, bronze, or clay.

WOODEN COFFINS FOR CATS

MUMMIFIED CAT

OFFERINGS ►
Dog mummies were offered to two gods: Anubis and Wepwawet. Both gods took the form of a jackal or dog. Anubis was the god of mummification. Wepwawet was the god who opened ways—he could open the way for a pharaoh's foreign conquests, for example. Anubis was worshiped at Hardai, which the Greeks renamed Cynopolis ("Dog City"). Wepwawet's temple was at Asyut, which the Greeks called Lykopolis ("Wolf City").

THE APIS BULL

The Egyptians believed that the creator god Ptah came to Earth in the form of a bull, worshiped as a god at Memphis. It is known as the Apis bull, the Greek form of its Egyptian name *Hap*. When an Apis bull died, the god was believed to transfer himself to another bull, which could be recognized by special markings on its coat, tail, and tongue. The dead Apis bull was mummified and laid to rest in a set of catacombs (underground burial chambers) called the Serapeum, at Saqqara.

Limestone relief from Thebes showing newborn bull calf

▲ ON PARADE

The Apis bull made public appearances at festivals. It was led on processions through the streets, and shown to the public at a ceremonial Window of Appearances, which was a feature of royal palaces. When people looked at the bull, they were certain that they were seeing a powerful, living god. Worshipers asked the bull for advice, and priests explained the bull's answers.

◄ A NEW APIS CALF

On the death of an Apis bull, newborn calves all over Egypt were examined to find one with the correct markings. The Egyptians believed that the animal was magically conceived when the god Ptah struck a particular cow with a bolt of lightning. As the mother of a god, this cow was also revered as sacred. She was cared for at the Apis temple, and mummified after her death.

Crown of the sacred bull

BRONZE STATUETTE OF A BUCHIS BULL

SACRED BULL CULTS ►

The Apis bull was one of several bull cults. The Buchis bull, for example, was believed to be the manifestation of the war god, Montu, and was worshiped in a temple at Hermonthis, south of Luxor. According to the Roman writer Macrobius, the bull changed color every hour, and had hair that grew backward. Buchis bulls were mummified and buried in an underground tomb, the Bucheum, discovered in 1927.

SACRED COWS

The Apis bull, and other bull and cow gods, were believed to help in the afterlife, where they could guide and protect the dead. In this papyrus, a dead man called Maiherperi is praying to several sacred cows and a bull, asking for their help. Each animal has its name written above it, and a table of offerings in front. The sacred animals listen attentively, their eyes fixed on Maiherperi.

The papyrus comes from a collection of spells buried with Maiherperi to help him on his journey to the next world. Maiherperi was a royal fan-bearer who died in his twenties around 1390 BC. His black skin tells us that he came from Nubia.

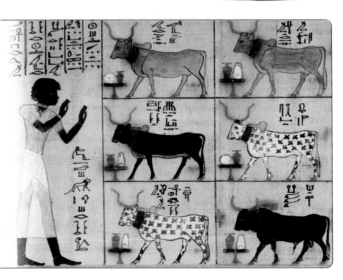

Niche for votive inscriptions

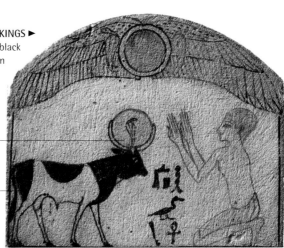

SACRED MARKINGS ►
According to the Greek writer Herodotus, the Apis bull was black with a white square on its forehead, the image of an eagle on its back, a scarab beetle under its tongue, and double hairs on its tail. However, stone tablets and paintings of Apis bulls show them to be black and white. This bull has an uraeus, a sacred protective cobra, standing between its horns.

e animal mummies

Disc of the sun god Ra

Apis bull with black and white markings

▼ THE APIS FUNERAL
Apis bulls were mummified and buried in massive stone sarcophagi in the Serapeum, which was built by Rameses II (who reigned from 1279 to 1213 BC). When the Serapeum was rediscovered in 1851, all but one of the sarcophagi were empty, robbed in ancient times. A second set of catacombs, found later in another part of the Serapeum, contained two more intact mummies. These catacombs contain niches cut into the walls, where worshipers left votive inscriptions—messages to the gods.

BULL CALF MUMMY
FROM 30 BC

Eyes painted on linen bandages

Linen bandages laid in decorative patterns

Body is wrapped to appear as if the calf is sitting down

Entrance to the catacombs of the mummified bulls

▲ MUMMIFIED BULL
Calves were mummified if they were the offspring of a sacred bull. The earliest surviving mummy of an Apis bull, dating from around 1300 BC, contained only the skull and broken bones of a bull. It has been suggested that the bull had been ceremonially eaten by the pharaoh and the priests. However, we know from writings that, at a later date, the bull was fully mummified.

EGYPT'S LAST MUMMIES

In 332 BC, King Alexander of Macedon conquered Egypt and was crowned pharaoh. Many of Alexander's Macedonian and Greek subjects settled in Egypt. They created a new civilization, combining Egyptian and Greek influences. This Hellenistic civilization continued under the Romans, who conquered Egypt in 30 BC. The mixture of influences can be seen in mummies of the period, which combine Egyptian mummification with realistic portraits of the deceased. These were the last Egyptian mummies, and they have given us perhaps the finest portrait paintings to survive from the ancient world.

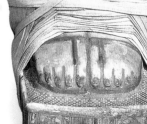

Each eyelash was painted individually

Gilded stucco buttons decorate the bandages

HORNS OF AMUN ▶
This coin shows Alexander wearing the curved ram's horns of Amun, whom he identified with the chief Greek god, Zeus. The Egyptians believed that the god Amun was the creator of all things. When Alexander was crowned pharaoh, the Egyptian priests hailed him as Son of Amun, which was one of the royal titles. Alexander, who had always believed that he was no ordinary human. He was delighted to be told that he was the son of a god.

mummies

A ROMAN BOY ▶
Unlike the Egyptians, the Romans had a long tradition of realistic portraiture, believing that it was important to preserve a dead person's likeness. This young boy's portrait was painted on a thin limewood panel, using paint made from beeswax and pigments. It was placed over his mummified face and secured with linen bandages, which have been carefully arranged to form decorative panels. The mummy dates from around AD 100 to 120.

Garland of roses held in the left hand

Dried poppy heads and ears of wheat held in the right hand

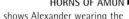

▲ COFFIN-LID PORTRAITS
The coffin lids of Roman mummies were sometimes decorated with painted plaster portraits. The head is always raised, as though resting on a pillow. This woman can be dated to AD 190–220 from her hairstyle and the mass of jewelry she wears. Her jewelry includes two wrist bangles of twisted gold, one gold bracelet, six rings, and three necklaces.

▲ PAINTED FROM DEATH?
Like most Roman mummy portraits, this young man (from AD 80 to 120) and woman (from AD 160 to 170) look healthy. People often assume that the portraits were painted during the subject's lifetime. But the age of the body often matches that shown in the portrait. Many portraits are of children, who would have died unexpectedly, before their portrait could be painted. So it is likely that many portraits were painted after death.

MUMMIFICATION IN THE ROMAN ERA

MUMMY SHROUD
This boy's mummy was given a full-length portrait, painted on a shroud (burial cloth). Since this was part of the burial equipment, it must have been painted after his death. The mantle and strange, tufted hairstyle date this mummy to AD 230–250. CT scans show that the boy died at the age of 8–10 years.

CRUDE MUMMIFICATION
Although late mummifiers took great care with the outer appearance of mummies, their preservation methods for the actual body were less sophisticated. Bodies, like this young girl's, were simply covered with large amounts of resin. Many were left to decompose before mummification took place.

▼ KOM AL-DIKKA ROMAN THEATER
The capital of Greek and Roman Egypt was Alexandria, the Mediterranean port founded by Alexander the Great. This theater, in the center of Alexandria, was built by the Romans. It is Roman in style, with straight columns instead of the curved columns found in Egyptian temples. The theater was used for plays, musical performances, and wrestling contests. The white marble for the seats was imported from Italy, and the green marble for the columns came from Asia Minor (modern-day Turkey). Egypt was now part of the wider Mediterranean world.

Marble seats for around 700–800 spectators

EMPEROR ENDS MUMMIFICATION
Once the Roman Empire became Christian, in the fourth century AD, the demand for mummification declined. Christians had their own idea of an afterlife, which did not require the preservation of their bodies.

A series of Christian emperors stamped out the old pagan religion, whose gods, such as Amun and Osiris, they saw as demons. The statues of the gods were smashed and Christian crosses were carved on the temple walls. Finally, in AD 392, Emperor Theodosius the Great (who reigned from 379 to 395 AD) banned all forms of pagan worship. By this time, the 3,000-year-old practice of making Egyptian mummies had probably already ended.

TOMB ROBBERS

The gold masks and amulets of royal mummies were intended to protect them. Yet these very treasures made them attractive to robbers. Almost all the royal tombs in the Valley of the Kings were plundered. Court records show that the tomb robbers worked in well-organized gangs, in groups of seven or eight men. These included stonemasons, to break open the royal sarcophagus, and a smith to melt down the stolen metals in his furnace. A boatman would wait by the Nile to take the robbers across the river to sell their treasures in the city of Thebes.

◀ VILLAGE OF THE TOMB-WORKERS
Deir el-Medina was home to the people who made the tombs in the Valley of the Kings. Many of the robbers were probably tomb workers. They had the advantage of knowing where the tombs were, since they had often built them themselves. To escape detection, they usually tunneled into a tomb from the rear, leaving the sealed tomb entrance intact.

WORKERS' TOOLS

The workers who lived in Deir el-Medina used the same tools to break into the royal tombs as they did to build them. The robbers used mallets and chisels to break open the stone sarcophagus, and saws to hack the gilding from coffins.

WOODEN MALLET

CHISEL   SAW   DRILL   ROPE

Weight of unsupported lid made it split in two

SARCOPHAGUS OF RAMESES IV ▶
The sarcophagus of Rameses IV (who reigned from c. 1153 to 1147 BC) had a massive granite lid. Unable to lift the lid, the robbers smashed a hole in its side. Later, tomb inspectors rescued the mummy, now stripped of its amulets, and rewrapped it. They then concealed it, along with the mummies of eight other pharaohs, in the tomb of Amenhotep II, where it was rediscovered in 1898 by European explorers.

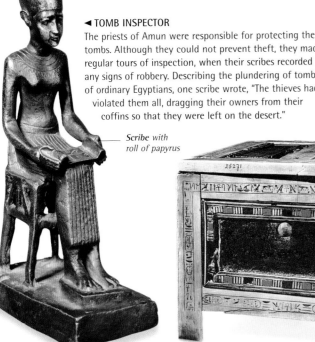

◄ TOMB INSPECTOR

The priests of Amun were responsible for protecting the
tombs. Although they could not prevent theft, they made
regular tours of inspection, when their scribes recorded
any signs of robbery. Describing the plundering of tombs
of ordinary Egyptians, one scribe wrote, "The thieves had
violated them all, dragging their owners from their
coffins so that they were left on the desert."

Scribe with
roll of papyrus

*Cheek and upper
part of face is
just skin—the
skull is missing*

*Head was
severed from
the body*

▲ PROTECTED TREASURE

When they learned that a royal tomb had been robbed,
the priests of Amun removed the mummy, along with any
treasures left by the robbers. This casket, with inlaid ivory
panels, was saved from the tomb of Rameses IX (who
reigned from c. 1126 to 1108 BC). It was placed, along with
40 royal mummies and many of their belongings, in a
secret tomb at Deir el-Bahri in the Valley of the Queens,
where it was rediscovered in 1881.

▲ TOMB POLICE

The tomb inspectors had the power to beat and torture suspected
thieves, to make them confess and name their accomplices. Many
confessions still survive, written on papyrus. One robber admitted,
"I have continued to this day the practice of robbing
the tombs of the nobles and the people of the land
who rest in the west. And a large number of other
people rob them as well."

tomb
robbers

RAMESES VI ▲

No royal mummy was more badly damaged
by tomb robbers than that of Rameses VI
(who reigned from c. 1143 to 1136 BC). When
it was discovered in 1898, the right arm and
the skull, except for the lower jaw, were
missing. Ancient restorers had attempted to
make Rameses look more like a mummy by
jumbling bones together. To make up for
missing bones, they included hands from
two other mummies, giving him three in all.

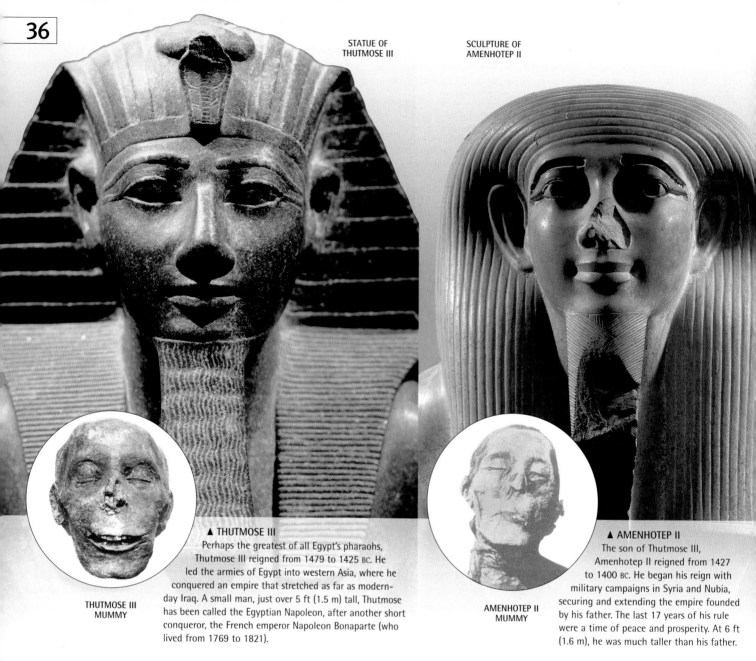

STATUE OF
THUTMOSE III

SCULPTURE OF
AMENHOTEP II

THUTMOSE III
MUMMY

▲ THUTMOSE III
Perhaps the greatest of all Egypt's pharaohs,
Thutmose III reigned from 1479 to 1425 BC. He
led the armies of Egypt into western Asia, where he
conquered an empire that stretched as far as modern-
day Iraq. A small man, just over 5 ft (1.5 m) tall, Thutmose
has been called the Egyptian Napoleon, after another short
conqueror, the French emperor Napoleon Bonaparte (who
lived from 1769 to 1821).

AMENHOTEP II
MUMMY

▲ AMENHOTEP II
The son of Thutmose III,
Amenhotep II reigned from 1427
to 1400 BC. He began his reign with
military campaigns in Syria and Nubia,
securing and extending the empire founded
by his father. The last 17 years of his rule
were a time of peace and prosperity. At 6 ft
(1.6 m), he was much taller than his father.

FAMOUS PHARAOHS

Around 1000 BC, the priests of Amun gathered the royal mummies
whose tombs had been robbed. They reburied the mummies in
two caches (hiding places). Thirteen were placed in the tomb of
Amenhotep II. Forty were hidden in a cliff tomb at Deir el-Bahri.
The pharaohs remained there, undisturbed, for almost 3,000 years,
only to be found by explorers in the 19th century. Thanks to this
amazing discovery, we can still look at the mummified faces of
some of the most famous rulers of the ancient world and compare
them to their stylized portraits on the statues.

◀ THUTMOSE THE BUILDER
Thutmose III used the wealth of the empire he had conquered to embark on
a great temple-building program. He expanded the temple of Amun at Karnak,
to the north of Thebes. Here, he set up this needle-shaped monument, called
an obelisk, in honor of Amun. The obelisk's point symbolized the sun's rays
and was originally gilded to make it gleam in the bright sun.

pharaohs

WOODEN
COFFIN OF SETI I

STATUE OF
RAMESES II

SETI I
MUMMY

RAMESES II
MUMMY

▲ SETI I

Seti I reigned from 1294 to 1279 BC. He successfully fought off a new threat from the expanding empire of the Hittites, who lived in what is now Turkey. The portrait above is painted on Seti's wooden coffin. Stripped of its original gold covering by thieves, the coffin was painted white by restorers, who then added the pharaoh's features in black. Seti has the best-preserved face of all the royal mummies.

▲ RAMESES THE GREAT

Coming to the throne in 1279 BC, Rameses II ruled Egypt for 66 years and fathered more than 100 sons. His unusually long reign gave him time to build an enormous number of temples and monuments. As a result of his many surviving statues, the face of Rameses is more familiar than any other pharaoh's. X-rays show that his worn teeth were in a terrible state by the time he died, with severe abscesses.

▲ STELLAR ART

Some of the finest Egyptian art dates from the reign of Seti I, including the wall paintings from his tomb in the Valley of the Kings. This painting, from the ceiling of his burial chamber, shows the constellations of the northern sky. The ox with the man behind it represents the Big Dipper (also called the Plow), whose stars are marked with red dots. Seti's empty tomb was discovered in 1817.

▲ BATTLE OF KADESH

The most famous event of Rameses's reign was a battle he fought against the Hittites around 1274 BC, at Kadesh, Syria. Rameses had accounts of the battle inscribed on the walls of his temples, where he showed himself triumphing over the Hittites, single-handedly shooting them down from his chariot with his bow and arrow. In fact, the battle resulted in a stalemate.

TUTANKHAMUN: THE SEARCH

In 1907, an archaeological team working for a wealthy US lawyer, Theodore Davis, discovered an undecorated tomb in the Valley of the Kings, the royal burial ground at Thebes, near Luxor. Nearby, there was a pit containing items bearing the name of a little-known pharaoh, Tutankhamun. Davis assumed that the undecorated tomb, long since robbed, had belonged to Tutankhamun. It seemed that all the royal burials had now been found and accounted for. But British archaeologist Howard Carter was unconvinced. In 1917, he began to search for Tutankhamun's tomb.

◄ HOWARD CARTER

By 1917, when he began his search, Howard Carter (1874–1939) had been working in Egypt for 26 years. He knew the Valley of the Kings better than anyone. Carter suspected that Tutankhamun's tomb lay in one particular area, which was piled high with heaps of ancient garbage. Carter later wrote, "I had reason to believe that the ground beneath had never been touched, and a strong conviction that we should find the tomb there."

Egyptian worker guards entrance to Tutankhamun's tomb.

THE VALLEY OF THE KINGS—THE ROYAL TOMBS

The Valley of the Kings contains 62 known tombs. Twenty belonged to the pharaohs who ruled Egypt from 1504 to 1085 BC. The rest held members of the royal family, or nobles, or had never been used. Of the pharaohs' tombs, most had been known about for centuries. Four were discovered between 1799 and 1817, and nine more between 1899 and 1903. Every single one was found robbed.

(A) Rameses II	(D) Amenmeses	(G) Rameses VI
(B) Seti I	(E) Rameses III	(H) Tutankhamun
(C) Rameses I	(F) Queen Tiy	(I) Mernapth

LORD CARNARVON ▶

Since 1909, Carter's excavations had been funded by Lord Carnarvon (1865–1923). Carnarvon had first come to Egypt in 1903 for the sake of his health, and became fascinated by the ancient civilization. From 1917 until 1921, Carnarvon spent a lot of money while Carter searched, without success, for Tutankhamun. With nothing to show for his investment, Carnarvon began to lose patience. He told Carter he would pay for just one more season's digging.

THE DIG ▶

Carnarvon's money went to pay 100 Egyptian laborers, who systematically cleared the area where Carter hoped to find the tomb. At last, on November 1, 1922, during the final digging season, Carter's workers uncovered a step cut into the rock. This was the first of 16 steps leading down to a doorway. The fact that the doorway had not been broken open raised Carter's hopes that the tomb beyond might have escaped robbery.

Entrance to tomb of Rameses VI

CARNARVON

CARTER

TO THE SECOND DOORWAY ▶

On November 6, Carter cabled Lord Carnarvon in England. "At last I have made a wonderful discovery in the Valley; a magnificent tomb with seals intact." Carter waited until Carnarvon arrived, on November 23, before opening the door. Beyond it, he found a sloping passageway, with a second sealed doorway at the far end. This photograph shows Carnarvon and Carter in front of the second doorway. They are about to make the greatest archaeological discovery in history.

◀ VISITORS ON SITE

News of the discovery of a new royal tomb caused an international sensation, and wealthy tourists quickly filled the upscale hotels of Luxor. On November 30, Carter wrote in his diary, "We were totally unprepared for such a large quantity of visitors." The stream of tourists, journalists, and officials slowed Carter's excavation. It took him almost a decade to examine the entire contents of the tomb. This photograph shows Carter and Carnarvon giving some of the first visitors a tour of the site.

Tutankhamun

THE TOMB

On November 26, 1922, Howard Carter stood at the end of the dark entrance corridor of the tomb he had discovered. He knocked a hole in the wall and pushed his candle into the space before him. What he saw was so astonishing that, for a moment, he could not speak. Standing beside him, Lord Carnarvon demanded, "Can you see anything?" "Yes," Carter replied, "wonderful things!" He could see a room packed with treasures, glittering with gold. This, however, was merely the antechamber of the tomb.

◄ THE SHRINE DOORS
When Carter entered the burial chamber in February 1923, he found that it was almost filled with a huge rectangular shrine of gilded wood. This was the first of four shrines that had to be dismantled and removed before Carter could reach the king's stone sarcophagus, containing three nested coffins. Here, he opens the richly decorated doors of the innermost shrine and finds the king's sarcophagus.

INSIDE THE ANTECHAMBER ►
Looking into the antechamber, Carter later recalled that his first impression was of "strange animals, statues and gold—everywhere the gilt of gold." There were almost two hundred objects, including three large, gilt couches with the heads of animals, 48 white, oval boxes containing joints of meat, four dismantled chariots, and various boxes containing jewelry, shaving equipment, games, and hunting equipment. It took Carter two years to photograph and record every item.

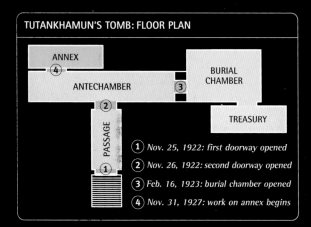

TUTANKHAMUN'S TOMB: FLOOR PLAN

ANNEX
④
ANTECHAMBER ③ BURIAL CHAMBER
②
PASSAGE
TREASURY
①

① Nov. 25, 1922: first doorway opened
② Nov. 26, 1922: second doorway opened
③ Feb. 16, 1923: burial chamber opened
④ Nov. 31, 1927: work on annex begins

PROTECTING THE PHARAOH ▲

The objects in the tomb served two main purposes. Many, such as this amulet, were there to give the pharaoh magical protection against the perils he would face on his journey to the next world. The amulet, called a wedjet, represents the right eye of the god Horus. It was found on the chest of King Tutankhamun's mummy. Other objects, such as joints of meat, loaves of bread, figs, and jars of beer, were there to supply the pharaoh's physical needs in the next world.

1. *Headboard* with goddess Ammut—part hippo, part lioness, and part crocodile

2. *Cross-legged stool* made of ebony wood decorated with ivory

3. *Wooden box* containing the king's shaving equipment

4. *Chair* made from papyrus and ebony

5. *Traveling box* decorated with strips of wood and gold inlay

6. *Bed* of white-washed wood with a woven linen mattress

7. *Second couch,* in the form of a cow—possibly the goddess Hathor

8. *Tail of third couch,* in the form of a lioness

9. *Oval boxes* containing joints of meat for the king to eat in the next world

10. *Treasure box* containing the remains of the king's jeweled corslet

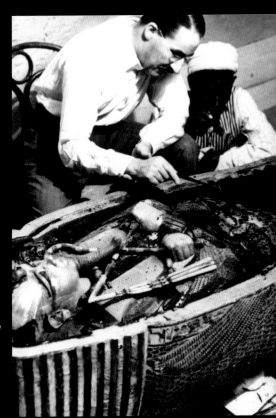

Tutankhamun

THE INNER COFFIN ▲

The inner coffin was stuck to the second one by a mass of dried, black resin— remnants of oils that had been poured over the coffin by the priests at the time of burial. Despite heating the coffins in the midday Egyptian sun, Carter was unable to separate them. In this picture, he is chipping away at the oil on top of the inner coffin, which still rests inside the second one, in order to raise its lid and expose the king's mummy.

THE BOY KING

Before Howard Carter discovered his tomb in 1922, almost nothing was known of the pharaoh Tutankhamun. The pharaoh had died in his late teens in 1327 BC. The treasures that Carter found in Tutankhamun's tomb were so magnificent that today the boy king has become the most famous pharaoh of all. Even so, we still know very little about his nine-year reign or how he met his death, or why he died at such a young age. One theory is that he was murdered by his successor, Ay, who married his widow and oversaw the burial.

◄ DESTROYER OF EVIL
This gilded wood statuette shows Tutankhamun hunting hippopotamus with a harpoon. His crown shows that this is a ceremonial and symbolic scene, not an image of a real hunt. The scene represents the pharaoh's role as the protector of order on Earth. The hippopotamus, which destroyed crops, stood for evil and disorder.

Skin damage caused during the unwrapping

Tutankhamun

THE FACE BENEATH THE MASK ►
The gold mask, attached to the king's head with dried resin, had to be heated in order to remove it. Carter then unwound the final wrappings to reveal the face of the king, which he described as, "a serene and placid countenance, that of a young man." Despite Carter's care, the head was damaged during the unwrapping, losing some skin and parts of the ears.

Nekhbet protects the pharaoh

False beard worn by pharaohs for ceremonial occasions

The wings of four protective goddesses (Isis, Nephthys, Nekhbet, and Wadjet) enclose the mummy

SOLID GOLD COFFIN ►
Tutankhamun's mummy had been placed in three beautifully made coffins, which fit one into another. The outer two were made of cedar, using wood brought from Lebanon. They were gilded with gold leaf and decorated with colored stones, such as turquoise. The inner coffin, shown here, was made of solid gold. It weighs 243 lb (110.4 kg) and is 74 in (188 cm) long.

Cartouche contains pharaoh's name

◄ THE ROYAL NAME
Carter could identify the pharaoh because his name was written on the walls of his tomb and on many of his treasures. This gold fan in the shape of a palm frond shows the royal names enclosed in two ovals, called cartouches. The king's name is protected by Nekhbet, the vulture goddess, who was the guardian of the pharaoh. The rim of the fan was originally decorated with ostrich feathers.

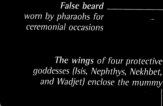

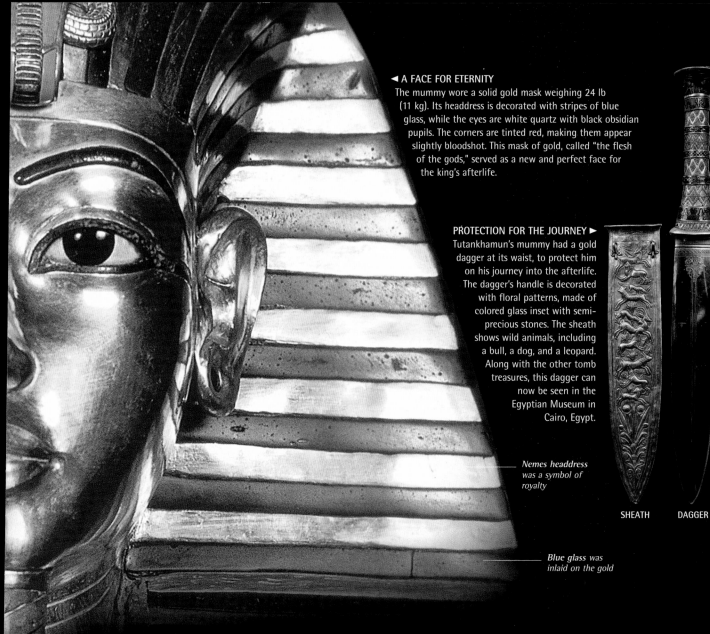

◄ A FACE FOR ETERNITY
The mummy wore a solid gold mask weighing 24 lb (11 kg). Its headdress is decorated with stripes of blue glass, while the eyes are white quartz with black obsidian pupils. The corners are tinted red, making them appear slightly bloodshot. This mask of gold, called "the flesh of the gods," served as a new and perfect face for the king's afterlife.

PROTECTION FOR THE JOURNEY ►
Tutankhamun's mummy had a gold dagger at its waist, to protect him on his journey into the afterlife. The dagger's handle is decorated with floral patterns, made of colored glass inset with semi-precious stones. The sheath shows wild animals, including a bull, a dog, and a leopard. Along with the other tomb treasures, this dagger can now be seen in the Egyptian Museum in Cairo, Egypt.

Nemes headdress was a symbol of royalty

SHEATH   DAGGER

Blue glass was inlaid on the gold

THE TOMB TODAY ▲
Tutankhamun's mummy has been put back inside his tomb at Thebes. It lies in his outermost coffin of gilded wood, protected beneath a sheet of glass. Of the many royal tombs open to the public in Egypt's Valley of the Kings, this is the only one still holding its original inhabitant.

REDISCOVERING EGYPT

Ever since the Greek traveler Herodotus visited Egypt around 500 BC, foreigners have been fascinated by mummies and the civilization that produced them. In the 12th century AD, Europeans prized mummies for their supposed benefits as medicine. It was only with Napoleon Bonaparte's invasion of Egypt in 1798 that a true understanding of the ancient civilization began to form. The 19th century saw the arrival of the first archaeologists, who searched for royal tombs and deciphered their ancient inscriptions.

FOR MEDICINAL USE ►
From the 12th to the 17th centuries, Europeans ate ground-up mummies as medicine. This was because of an Arabic book praising the medicinal use of bitumen, which people mistakenly thought was used in mummification. The word mummy comes from *mummiya*, the Arabic name for bitumen. The mummies were shipped from Egypt in large numbers to be made into medicine by apothecaries (pharmacists).

◄ NAPOLEON IN EGYPT
In 1798, French general Napoleon Bonaparte invaded Egypt, which the French occupied until 1802. Along with his soldiers, Napoleon took a team of scholars, engineers, and artists who measured and recorded the monuments of the country. Napoleon was particularly fascinated by the three pyramids at Giza. He calculated that they contained enough stone to build a wall 10 ft (3 m) high and 1 ft (30 cm) wide around all of France.

◄ FRENCH SURVEYS
Back in France, the material collected by Napoleon's surveyors was published in a series of volumes called *Description de l'Égypte*, including some 3,000 illustrations. This one shows surveyors measuring the Great Sphinx, still buried up to its neck under desert sand. Across Europe, the publication led to a new fascination with ancient Egypt among historians and the general public alike.

Hieroglyphs are inscribed at the top of the stone

THE ROSETTA STONE ►
In 1799, Napoleon's soldiers discovered a basalt stone at Rosetta. The Rosetta Stone was inscribed with a priestly decree, written in hieroglyphs, Greek, and Demotic (an Egyptian language). By comparing the hieroglyphs with the other texts, French scholar Jean-Francois Champollion (1790–1832) began to decipher hieroglyphs, which had fallen out of use in the 4th century AD. In 1828, he published the first real breakthrough in deciphering hieroglyphs – now they could be read again.

COLLECTORS' ITEMS ►
By the 19th century, mummies such as this head were sought after by private collectors in Europe and the US. In the 1830s, English collector Thomas Pettigrew held a series of mummy unrollings for paying audiences. Spectators would watch as "Mummy Pettigrew" stripped an Egyptian mummy of its bandages. In 1852, he turned the dead Duke of Hamilton into a mummy, following a request in the duke's will.

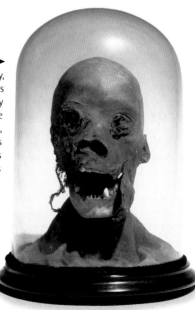

Wings inlaid with precious stones, such as blue lapis lazuli

Scarab holds a disk representing Re or Ra, the sun god

▲ ART DECO JEWELRY DESIGN

The discovery of Tutankhamun's tomb and treasures led to a fresh craze for ancient Egypt, nicknamed "Tutmania." Egypt influenced a new style of decorative arts called Art Deco. This was named after the *Exposition Internationale des Arts Décoratifs*, the 1925 Paris trade fair where the style first appeared. Art Deco brooches, such as this scarab, are closely modeled on the colorful jewelry found with Tutankhamun.

rediscovery

TUTANKHAMUN'S CURSE ▶

In April 1923, only two months after entering the burial chamber of Tutankhamun, Lord Carnarvon, who had funded the excavation, died from an infected mosquito bite. This led to rumors that he was the victim of an ancient curse. It was claimed that an inscription above the tomb doorway read, "Death shall come on swift wings to him that toucheth the tomb of the Pharaoh." In fact, no such inscription exists.

▲ MUMMIES IN THE MOVIES

Tutmania inspired a 1932 horror movie, *The Mummy*. The film stars Boris Karloff as Imhotep, an ancient Egyptian priest who had been buried alive for his crimes against the gods. A British archaeologist discovers his mummy and brings him back to life by reading a magic scroll. The mummy then stalks the streets of Cairo, searching for a woman he believes to be the reincarnation of his long-dead love.

Walls are decorated with scenes from Egyptian tomb paintings

DESIGN AND ARCHITECTURE ▶

Tutmania influenced architecture as well as jewelry. In 1924, during the height of the craze, Harman and Louis Peery built Peery's Egyptian Cinema in Ogden, Utah. The columns are based on those found in Egyptian temples, which were modeled on bundles of papyrus and are colored as brightly as Egyptian jewelry. Restored and reopened in 1997, the theater still gives visitors the feeling that they have been transported to ancient Egypt.

MUMMY DETECTIVES

Scientists who investigate mummies are like detectives, collecting clues to discover how a mummy lived and died. Until recently, the only way to examine a mummy was to unwrap its bandages and cut it open. Today, however, scientists use nondestructive techniques, such as endoscopy and CT (computed tomography) scanning to examine mummies. They can now learn many things about the mummies without damaging them—including their age, medical history, family relationships, and sometimes even the cause of their death.

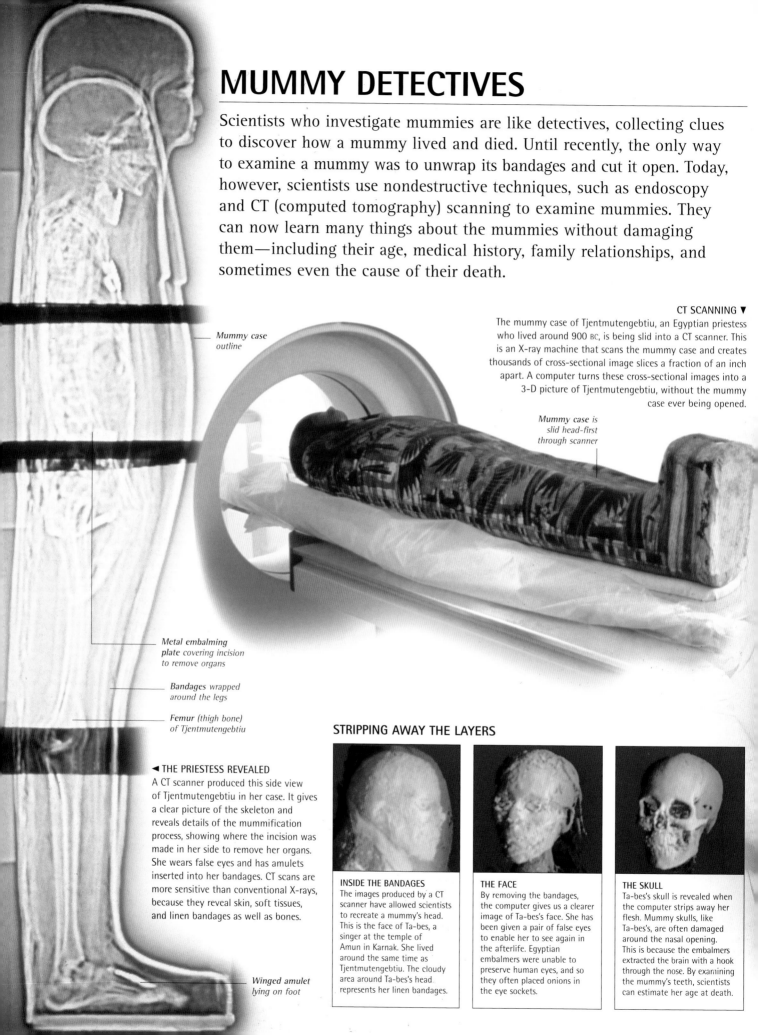

Mummy case outline

CT SCANNING ▼
The mummy case of Tjentmutengebtiu, an Egyptian priestess who lived around 900 BC, is being slid into a CT scanner. This is an X-ray machine that scans the mummy case and creates thousands of cross-sectional image slices a fraction of an inch apart. A computer turns these cross-sectional images into a 3-D picture of Tjentmutengebtiu, without the mummy case ever being opened.

Mummy case is slid head-first through scanner

Metal embalming plate covering incision to remove organs

Bandages wrapped around the legs

Femur (thigh bone) of Tjentmutengebtiu

◄ THE PRIESTESS REVEALED
A CT scanner produced this side view of Tjentmutengebtiu in her case. It gives a clear picture of the skeleton and reveals details of the mummification process, showing where the incision was made in her side to remove her organs. She wears false eyes and has amulets inserted into her bandages. CT scans are more sensitive than conventional X-rays, because they reveal skin, soft tissues, and linen bandages as well as bones.

Winged amulet lying on foot

STRIPPING AWAY THE LAYERS

INSIDE THE BANDAGES
The images produced by a CT scanner have allowed scientists to recreate a mummy's head. This is the face of Ta-bes, a singer at the temple of Amun in Karnak. She lived around the same time as Tjentmutengebtiu. The cloudy area around Ta-bes's head represents her linen bandages.

THE FACE
By removing the bandages, the computer gives us a clearer image of Ta-bes's face. She has been given a pair of false eyes to enable her to see again in the afterlife. Egyptian embalmers were unable to preserve human eyes, and so they often placed onions in the eye sockets.

THE SKULL
Ta-bes's skull is revealed when the computer strips away her flesh. Mummy skulls, like Ta-bes's, are often damaged around the nasal opening. This is because the embalmers extracted the brain with a hook through the nose. By examining the mummy's teeth, scientists can estimate her age at death.

STUDYING MUMMY TISSUE

TISSUE SAMPLING
This scientist is removing a sample of tissue from a mummy's foot, in order to extract DNA (deoxyribonucleic acid). DNA carries the mummy's genetic code—the set of instructions for building cells, unique to every individual. The scientist wears latex gloves so her own DNA does not contaminate the sample.

DNA PROFILING
A computer translates the genetic code into a printout called a DNA profile, which resembles a bar code. By comparing the DNA of different mummies, we may be able to discover if and how they are related. However, ancient DNA is often broken into small pieces, making comparisons difficult.

MICROSCOPIC STUDY
Scientists use powerful microscopes to examine tissues and diagnose diseases. Here, a thin slice of a mummy's liver, stained to make it more visible, has been projected onto a monitor using a video light microscope. Such studies reveal that many Egyptians suffered from a disease called schistosomiasis.

PARASITE
A parasitic worm living in the waters of the Nile causes schistosomiasis. Scientists are building up a profile of the disease since ancient times, using tissues from hundreds of mummies. They hope this will help in the modern treatment of schistosomiasis, which affects 250 million people worldwide.

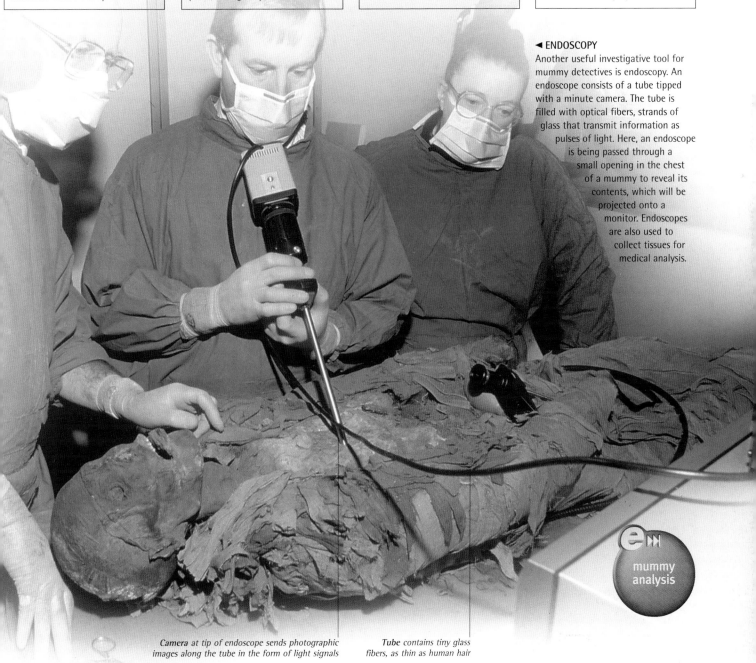

◄ ENDOSCOPY
Another useful investigative tool for mummy detectives is endoscopy. An endoscope consists of a tube tipped with a minute camera. The tube is filled with optical fibers, strands of glass that transmit information as pulses of light. Here, an endoscope is being passed through a small opening in the chest of a mummy to reveal its contents, which will be projected onto a monitor. Endoscopes are also used to collect tissues for medical analysis.

Camera at tip of endoscope sends photographic images along the tube in the form of light signals

Tube contains tiny glass fibers, as thin as human hair

mummy analysis

DATING METHODS

Archaeologists date finds so that they can compare objects from the same period. They use two main methods: relative and absolute dating. Relative dating determines the age of one object in relation to another. For example, finds from the lowest levels of archaeological digs are usually older than those higher up. Absolute dating tells us the actual age of a find without making a comparison. For example, coins can be dated absolutely because they have dates written on them. But it was not until the invention of carbon dating in 1949 that all objects could be given absolute dates.

mummy analysis

COMPARATIVE DATING ▶
Relative dating can be done on the basis of the style of an object. These two mummy masks are clearly ancient Egyptian, and a non-expert might assume they are the same age. In fact, the gold mask is around 1,000 years older than the painted one. More crudely made, the painted mask dates from a late period, when many Romans lived in Egypt. During this late period, the style of mummy masks was influenced by Roman art. More ordinary people were being mummified, and standards of mask-making were declining.

Nemes headdress shows this maks dates to the time of the pharaohs

Gold mask of Pharaoh Psusennes I (1040–999 BC)

Pink colouring is found on later masks

Cartonnage mummy mask, made some time after 30 BC

EARLY MASK

LATE MASK

CARBON DATING IN NATURE

CARBON
The sixth most common element in the universe is carbon. It can combine with other elements in so many ways that all living things contains carbon. This image is part of a model of a carbon molecule in which 80 carbon atoms join together to form a cage. An atom is the smallest particle of carbon—a period contains 10 million million atoms.

ABSORBING CARBON
Every living thing takes in carbon. Plants absorb it in the form of carbon dioxide from the atmosphere, and animals get their carbon by eating plants or plant-eating animals. When plants and animals die, they stop absorbing carbon. There are three isotopes (types of atom) known as Carbon 12, Carbon 13, and Carbon 14.

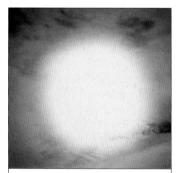

RADIOACTIVE CARBON
The most common isotopes, Carbon 12 and Carbon 13, are both stable—they remain in the same state. Carbon 14, which is much rarer, is unstable or radioactive as a result of radiation from the sun and outer space. Its atoms break down, at a known rate, called a half-life, to form another substance, Nitrogen 14.

WILLARD LIBBY
In 1949, American chemist Willard Libby first used Carbon 14 as a method of dating remains. The half-life of Carbon 14 is 5,730 years. This means it takes 5,730 years for half of its original atoms to decay. An ancient bone containing half the expected levels of Carbon 14 would therefore be 5,730 years old.

CARBON DATING A SPECIMEN

CALIBRATING A SAMPLE

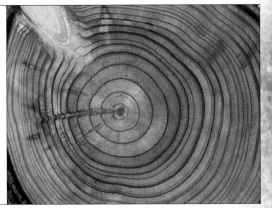

How much Carbon 14 is present in nature varies over time, so dating results must be calibrated (adjusted). To do this, scientists use the growth rings of bristlecone pine trees, which are the oldest living things on Earth. For each year of its life, a tree produces a growth ring, so a tree with 100 growth rings is 100 years old. By comparing the carbon dates of growth rings with their known age, scientists can work out what adjustments need to be made for other samples.

TAKING A SAMPLE

In order to date a find, such as this reindeer bone, a scientist must first remove a small sample. This piece of bone will be destroyed in the dating process—fortunately, only a few milligrams of bone are needed. The sample is soaked in acid to remove any other organic materials, such as soil, which may contain Carbon 14. If soil was left on the bone, the scientist would not obtain an accurate date. The sample is burned to make pure carbon, which can then be measured.

USING A SPECTROMETER

The carbon is placed in an Accelerator Mass Spectrometer and bombarded with cesium particles to produce a stream of particles. The stream is analyzed by the spectrometer, which can detect individual Carbon 14 atoms by the speed at which they move. When carbon dating was first introduced, scientists needed a relatively large sample to date a find. Now, thanks to sophisticated spectrometers, only a few milligrams are needed to date a sample.

DATING THE CHINCHORRO ▶

Carbon dating is especially useful when a previously unknown civilization is discovered. In 1917, a group of mummies unlike any ever seen before were found at Chinchorro Beach, Chile. Max Uhle, the German archaeologist who first studied them, estimated that they were about 2,000 years old. Thanks to carbon dating, we now know that the earliest are more than 7,000 years old, making them the oldest artificially-made mummies in the world.

Black paint
originally covered
the entire body

THE OLDEST MUMMIES

The oldest intentionally made mummies in the world are those of the Chinchorro people, who lived on the South American coast, in what is now northern Chile. More than 7,000 years ago, the Chinchorro were preserving their dead with methods even more elaborate than those of ancient Egypt. Before these mummies were first discovered, in 1917, it was thought that elaborate mummification was a feature of only rich societies, with kings and nobles. The Chinchorro, however, were simple hunting and fishing people.

ATACAMA DESERT, CHILE	
PERIOD:	c. 5050 BC–c. 2000 BC
DISCOVERED:	1917
BODY COUNT:	282 mummies so far

FAMILY BURIAL ▶

This group of mummies was excavated in 1983 at Arica, Chile. Like other Chinchorro mummies, they were reinforced with sticks, making them rigid objects that could stand upright. Many of the mummies show signs of repainting and repair. This suggests that they were kept among the living for some time before burial, perhaps leaning against the walls of houses. At some later date they were buried, often in family groups, along with grave goods such as fishhooks and whalebones.

Chinchorro

Clay mask with closed eyes, as if asleep

Grave goods

MUMMIES OF THREE CHILDREN

NATURAL MUMMIFICATION ▶
The hand on this child mummy has been preserved naturally in the desert. The Atacama Desert, where the Chinchorro buried their dead, is one of the driest places on Earth, and is perfectly suited for preserving human bodies. The oldest bodies found here date back to 8000 BC, and had mummified naturally. The Chinchorro people probably noticed that their dead remained intact and well-preserved in their graves, and then decided to improve their appearance.

Reed wrapping still covers the child's body

Fingernails are still intact

▲ BLACK PERIOD (5050 BC–2500 BC)
Some time before 5000 bc, the Chinchorro began to make clay masks for their dead. They painted them black, using grains of manganese sifted from beach sand. They also took the bodies apart. They saved the skin and the skeletons, which they stiffened with sticks. After packing grass, clay, and feathers around the frames, they replaced the skin, adding patches of sea lion skin. Then they covered the bodies with paste made from ash.

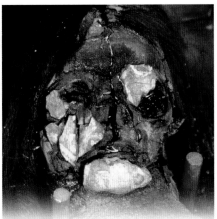

Clay mask painted with red ocher

◀ RED PERIOD (2500 BC–2000 BC)
The mask style changed around 2500 BC. The eyes and mouth were open, as if the dead were awake. The paint also changed from black manganese to red ocher. Instead of taking a body apart, the Chinchorro made cuts in the sides, to remove the organs. Then they stuffed the cavities with reeds, clay, and fur.

Ruptured skull where the brain was removed

Frame made from whalebone

Breasts modeled in ash paste

Body covered in ash paste

Wrapping made of reeds

▲ BABY MUMMY
The earliest artificial mummies discovered are of very young children. Perhaps they were mummified for grieving mothers who could not bear to be parted from them. The Chinchorro were unusual in that they even mummified stillborn fetuses. They may have believed they were giving these children a second chance—a new life as a mummy.

PERUVIAN MUMMIES

For more than 2,000 years, from around 500 BC to the 1570s, the peoples of Peru mummified their dead. Civilizations rose and fell, yet their mummification method continued with little change. Bodies were wrapped in bundles of cloth in a squatting position, knees drawn up to the chin, in the same way that native South Americans still sit to relax today. This posture helped preservation, by allowing bodily fluids to drain downward, out of the body. Mummies have been found throughout Peru, from the dry coastal deserts to the rugged Andes mountains and the lush rainforest.

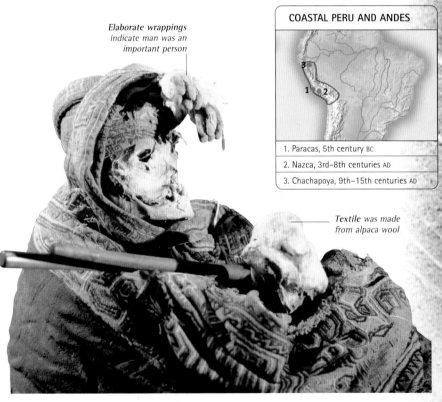

Elaborate wrappings indicate man was an important person

COASTAL PERU AND ANDES

1. Paracas, 5th century BC
2. Nazca, 3rd–8th centuries AD
3. Chachapoya, 9th–15th centuries AD

Textile was made from alpaca wool

▲ PARACAS MUMMY
The oldest known Peruvian mummies were found in the 1920s, on the peninsula of Paracas in Peru. There were 429 mummies, almost all elderly men, dating from the 5th century BC. They were wrapped in many layers of textiles. The textiles were part of the mummification procedure because they soaked up bodily moisture and speeded up the drying process.

◄ PARACAS TEXTILES
Paracas textiles are some of the most astonishing and beautiful ever made. Woven on huge looms, they are vividly colored and often depict strange animals. This textile shows a creature wearing an elaborate headdress and holding a snake. Such textiles would have been grave goods, symbols of status for the dead to take into the next life. One mummy was buried with 56 items of clothing, including 13 turbans.

THE NAZCA LINES ►
South of Paracas lies the Nazca desert, famous for its huge and mysterious figures, etched into the ground. They were made by the Nazca people, who lived in this area between 200 BC and AD 600. The figures, such as this 180-ft- (55-m-) long monkey, were created by clearing away the dark upper soil to reveal the lighter soil underneath. Nobody knows why the Nazca people made them. The complete images can only be seen from above, but there are no hills nearby, so the Nazca people must have seen them only in their imagination. Perhaps they were offerings to the gods. Burial sites have been discovered nearby, suggesting this may have been a sacred place.

◄ LOOTED NAZCA TOMBS
Near the Nazca figures there are cemeteries containing thousands of mummies, dating from AD 200 to 700. The dead buried here may be the very same people who made the desert figures, since their pottery is decorated with similar designs. Many of these cemeteries have now been looted. The mummy bundles contain valuable pottery and other grave goods that can be sold worldwide.

THE CLOUD PEOPLE OF PERU ►
In 1996, more than 200 mummies were found on a cliff ledge in the mountains of northern Peru. They were found in high cloud forest, a type of forest that is cool and wet because it is often immersed in clouds. The people who made these mummies sought out dry caves to preserve their dead. The Incas called these people the Chachapoya, which is thought to mean "cloud people."

Peru

▲ EXAMINING THE CHACHAPOYA
Close study shows that the earliest Chachapoya mummies, from the 9th century AD, were left to dry out naturally. In the 15th century, the Chachapoya began to embalm their dead by removing inner organs and tanning the skin. To make their features lifelike, they stuffed the mummy faces with cotton. Scientists are also identifying diseases from which the Chachapoya suffered, including spinal tuberculosis.

False head: the real head is inside the bundle

THE INCA EMPIRE

The ancient Peruvians had no writing system. To understand why they mummified their dead, we rely on accounts written down by Spaniards, who conquered Peru in the 1530s. At that time, the country was at the heart of the Inca empire, which stretched 2,500 miles (4,000 km) north to south. According to Spanish accounts, the Incas believed that the preserved dead were powerful spirits who could help the living, if their mummies were cared for. The Inca word for mummy means "something carefully kept."

◄ **CHIMU MUMMY**
This mummy was made by the Chimu, a people who had their own empire in Peru until they were conquered by the Incas in 1476. The Incas and the Chimu both mummified their dead by wrapping them in bundles of cloth. The mummies of ordinary people were often buried, but the mummies of rulers were kept in their palaces, where servants fanned them to keep them cool and offered them food and drink.

INCA EMPIRE, SOUTH AMERICA

| 1. Chan Chan, Chimu capital |
| 2. Puruchuco, Inca cemetery |
| 3. Cuzco, Inca capital |

Layers of fine cotton and wool cloth conceal a crouching body

GRAVE GOODS ►
Many of the peoples under Inca rule included grave goods in their mummy bundles, such as this little doll. Other goods include pottery vessels and precious metalwork, such as silver figurines and cups. The mummy bundles were placed in different locations. According to a Spanish writer, Pedro Cieza de Leon, the mummified dead were disposed of in various ways—some on high hills, others in their houses, and others in ancestral tombs.

CHIMU PALACE
These are the decorated mud-brick walls of a royal palace in the Chimu capital, Chan Chan. It was a huge city, with 10,000 dwellings, and nine large palaces, the homes of mummified Chimu rulers. When a ruler died, his successor had to build himself a new palace, for the previous one belonged to the dead. This custom was continued by the Incas.

▲ **CHIMU METALWORK**
The Chimu were the most skilled metalworkers in Peru, and made silver vessels with distinctive wide eyes and hooked noses. After conquering the Chimu empire, the Incas resettled the Chimu metalworkers in Cuzco, the Inca capital. The Chimu were then required to work for the Incas.

Incas

SPANISH CONQUISTADORS

This 16th-century print depicts the Spanish conquistadors ("conquerors") taking control of the Inca empire after capturing an Inca ruler. As Christians, they saw the Incas' care of mummies as the worship of false idols. They ordered the Incas to bury their dead without mummification, and evicted the royal mummies from their palaces in Cuzco. The Spanish chronicler Garcilaso de la Vega wrote: "They carried them in white shrouds through the streets and plazas, the Indians dropping to their knees, making reverence with groans and tears."

◄ ROYAL MUMMIES

Although no royal mummies survive, these Inca silver figurines with their elaborate headdresses help us imagine what the mummies might have looked like. Unlike the mummy bundles, the royal mummies had their faces open to the air so that they could eat and drink. According to Spaniard Garcilaso de la Vega, who saw the mummies, "Their bodies were so intact that they lacked neither hair, eyebrows, nor eyelashes."

MACHU PICCHU

The Incas were mountain people, living high in the Andes. Machu Picchu, an Inca ceremonial site 50 miles (80 km) from Cuzco and deep in the mountains, was never discovered by the Spaniards. Yet the site was abandoned around the time of the Spanish conquest. This was probably as a result of the breakdown of Inca society, devastated by war and diseases brought by the Spaniards. Machu Picchu was not rediscovered until 1911.

▲ PURUCHUCO UNWRAPPING

Here you can see the unwrapping of the mummy of a young woman, whose bundle also contained her two babies. They were found in 1999 in a vast Inca cemetery at Puruchuco, outside Lima, the modern capital of Peru. So far, more than 2,200 mummy bundles have been uncovered, dating from 1438 to 1530. The whole cemetery may contain 15,000 people, showing a large cross-section of Inca society. Personal belongings, such as food and everyday utensils, were discovered with the mummies.

INCA ICE MUMMIES

Some of the world's most spectacular mummy finds come from the Andes mountains. Since 1980, US explorer Johan Reinhard has made more than a hundred ascents in the Andes, discovering 40 Inca ritual sites. His most important discoveries include 18 mummified children, naturally frozen. The children had been taken high up into the mountains to be sacrificed to the Inca gods. Early Spanish accounts described these mountain sacrifices of children, called *capacochas*. The children were both gifts and messengers, sent by the Incas to ask the gods for help.

▲ REMAINS OF THE ROYAL CITY
This is Sacsayhuaman, the remains of fortifications that were once part of the Inca city at Cuzco. In this royal city, the sacrificial children were introduced to Inca rulers and honored with a large feast, before starting the procession to the mountaintop. The mountains were seen as powerful gods whose good will had to be won. The rain for crops came from the mountains, as did storms, volcanic eruptions, and avalanches.

Incas

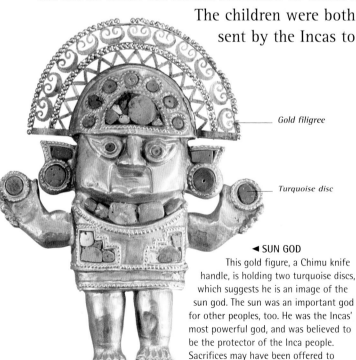

Gold filigree

Turquoise disc

◄ SUN GOD
This gold figure, a Chimu knife handle, is holding two turquoise discs, which suggests he is an image of the sun god. The sun was an important god for other peoples, too. He was the Incas' most powerful god, and was believed to be the protector of the Inca people. Sacrifices may have been offered to the sun as well as the mountain gods.

REINHARD'S MOUNTAIN SEARCH

INCA SHELTER
Reinhard located the ice mummies by following the trail of remains left by the Inca procession, such as this stone shelter. On their way up the mountain, the Incas built camps where they could rest at night and shelter from the freezing winds. At the summit, Reinhard found platforms enclosed by stones, where the children were sacrificed.

MUMMY DISCOVERY
This picture shows the discovery of a mummy on a mountain summit. Freezing temperatures and thin air make it difficult to climb in the Andes and dig for mummies. Reinhard relied on a team of native Peruvian climbers. Like the Incas, they are adapted to life at high altitudes, with larger-than-average lungs.

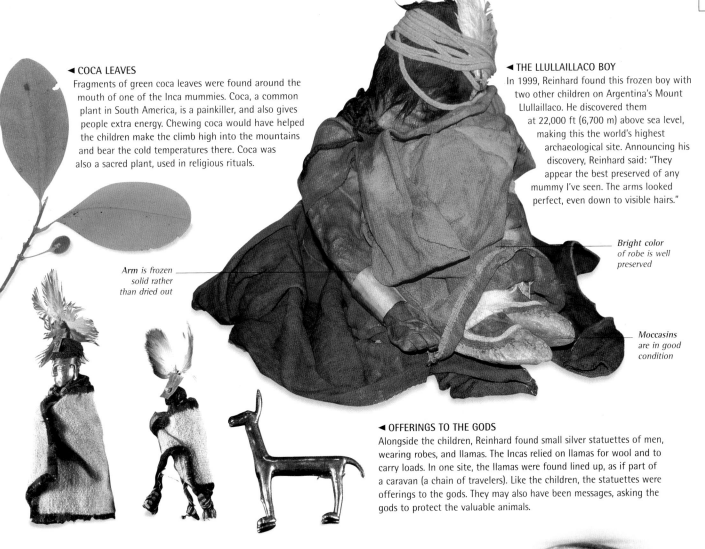

◄ COCA LEAVES

Fragments of green coca leaves were found around the mouth of one of the Inca mummies. Coca, a common plant in South America, is a painkiller, and also gives people extra energy. Chewing coca would have helped the children make the climb high into the mountains and bear the cold temperatures there. Coca was also a sacred plant, used in religious rituals.

◄ THE LLULLAILLACO BOY

In 1999, Reinhard found this frozen boy with two other children on Argentina's Mount Llullaillaco. He discovered them at 22,000 ft (6,700 m) above sea level, making this the world's highest archaeological site. Announcing his discovery, Reinhard said: "They appear the best preserved of any mummy I've seen. The arms looked perfect, even down to visible hairs."

Arm is frozen solid rather than dried out

Bright color of robe is well preserved

Moccasins are in good condition

◄ OFFERINGS TO THE GODS

Alongside the children, Reinhard found small silver statuettes of men, wearing robes, and llamas. The Incas relied on llamas for wool and to carry loads. In one site, the llamas were found lined up, as if part of a caravan (a chain of travelers). Like the children, the statuettes were offerings to the gods. They may also have been messages, asking the gods to protect the valuable animals.

"JUANITA" ►

In 1995, Reinhard accidentally discovered the frozen mummy of a 14-year-old girl, nicknamed "Juanita," while climbing Mount Ampato in Peru. CT scans showed that she had received a heavy blow to the right side of the head. This may have caused her death, or she may have died later, when her body fell down the mountainside. Her internal organs, hair, and blood were well preserved, as if she had died recently. She died about 500 years ago.

Fine wool garment indicates Juanita belonged to an important family

Ice keeps mummy preserved in museum

HEAD-HUNTERS

Throughout history, different warring peoples all over the world have removed the heads of defeated enemies and kept them as trophies. The most famous of these warriors are the Jivaro people, who still live in the rainforest of Ecuador. What made the Jivaro unique among head-hunters was their method of preserving a head by removing the skin and shrinking it. This created a gruesome trophy about the size of an orange, called a *tsantsa*. The Jivaro made a *tsantsa* to capture an enemy's spirit, which they believed would make its possessor more powerful.

ECUADORIAN RAINFOREST

PEOPLE:	Jivaro
TECHNIQUE:	head-shrinking
FIRST STUDIED:	19th century

◀ JIVARO TSANTSA

The Jivaro made *tsantsa*s to avenge wrongs committed by members of another tribe. They believed that failure to avenge dead ancestors would anger them, and bring bad luck. In making the *tsantsa*, a Jivaro head-hunter had to protect himself from the spirit of the dead person by sewing up the eyes and lips of the head. According to their beliefs, this would trap the spirit inside and prevent it from seeing and speaking.

REPLICA TSANTSA ▶

When experts compare the nose of this *tsantsa* with that of a genuine *tsantsa*, they can tell it is a fake. Western people have been fascinated by shrunken heads ever since they first discovered the Jivaro in the 19th century. To meet the demand from collectors and museums, taxidermists have created many replica *tsantsa*s, using goat or monkey skin, or bodies stolen from morgues. This replica is made from goat skin.

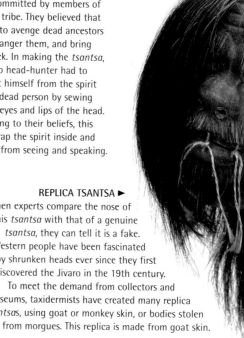

e▸▸
head hunters

◀ ECUADORIAN RAINFOREST

This is the rainforest of Ecuador, where the Jivaro people still live in many different tribes. Until the 20th century, these tribes lived in a constant state of warfare. Every head-hunting raid had to be avenged. The result was a bloody cycle of revenge killings, which forced the tribes to live in fortified villages. Jivaro men always carried weapons, for hunting and defense against raiders.

MAKING AND USING A TSANTSA

SHRINKING

After removing the skull, the Jivaro scraped the flesh off the skin and sewed the eyes and mouth shut. Then they boiled the skin for almost two hours in a mixture of herbs and water. This began the shrinking process. The Jivaro completed the *tsantsa* by filling the skin with heated sand and pebbles.

TEACHING

This Jivaro elder, photographed in the 1950s, is using a *tsantsa* to teach his sons to hate and fear their enemies. From a young age, boys were told that it was their duty to avenge their ancestors by hunting for heads. The more heads they took, the greater their reputation would be.

DISPLAY

The Jivaro displayed *tsantsa*s on the walls of houses, and wore them around their necks on special occasions. During ceremonial feasts, the warriors danced while brandishing their *tsantsa*s and reenacting successful raids. They did this to impress their tribe, and to please the spirits of ancestors.

MEXICAN MUMMIES

The Aztec people of Mexico used to sacrifice their enemies and display their skulls in vast numbers as trophies of war. The Spanish Conquest of the 1520s put an end to this, but the idea of viewing the dead continues in a festival known as the Day of the Dead, when people display *calavera*s (skeletons) in every Mexican town and village. This is regarded as a happy time, when the souls of the dead return to be with their living relatives. People can also come face to face with death by visiting the natural mummies on display at a museum in the Mexican town of Guanajuato.

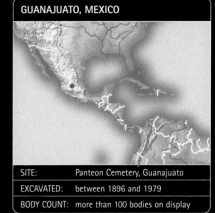

GUANAJUATO, MEXICO

SITE:	Panteon Cemetery, Guanajuato
EXCAVATED:	between 1896 and 1979
BODY COUNT:	more than 100 bodies on display

e ▸▸ Mexican mummies

◄ CALAVERA PUPPETS
Mexicans hold their Day of the Dead festivities on two Catholic holy days, All Saints Day and All Souls Day (1 and 2 November). On these days, they visit cemeteries to picnic with their departed loved ones, and give each other *calavera*s—dolls and candies shaped like skeletons. They also make puppet skeletons, out of wood or papier mâché, and dance them around. The skeletons are usually smiling, because Mexicans believe that the dead have returned to have fun, not to frighten.

Puppet calavera has movable limbs for dancing

PANTEON CEMETERY AND MUSEUM

CEMETERY VAULTS
One mummy lies on top of this pile of skulls and bones, stored inside the Panteon Cemetery vaults. Many of the bodies buried here were dug up between 1896 and 1979, when their relatives could no longer afford to pay a fee charged for space in the cemetery. As this picture shows, not all of the bodies had been mummified.

CLOTHED MUMMIES
More than 100 well-preserved mummies are on display, in glass cases, at the Panteon museum. Some are clothed, and others are naked or wearing only their shoes. Some of the bodies hold cards with philosophical statements, such as, "This is how you see my life; this is how I see the truth."

GUANAJUATO MUMMY ►
This is one of the mummies that were once buried in the Panteon Cemetery, Guanajuato. Minerals in the cemetery's dry soil may have preserved the bodies naturally. Many have their eyes open and mouth gaping. This is a result of rigor mortis, the stiffening and contraction of muscles that occurs after death. It shows that the bodies were not embalmed. One of the first things an embalmer does is to close the eyes and mouth of a dead person.

Words of wisdom for museum visitors to read

AN ARCTIC MYSTERY

In 1845, the English explorer Sir John Franklin sailed into the Canadian Arctic with two ships and 128 men. They never returned. In 1984, the bodies of three sailors were dug out of graves on Beechey Island in the Arctic Ocean. They had been buried deep in the frozen ground, where the cold preserved them perfectly. The sailors were examined to discover how they had died, in the hope that this might help solve one of the greatest mysteries in the history of exploration: what happened to the Franklin expedition?

▲ SIR JOHN FRANKLIN

This is a bronze plaque of Sir John Franklin. His mission was to find the Northwest Passage, a navigable route over the top of America from the Atlantic to the Pacific oceans. It had been a goal of European explorers ever since the 16th century, and many ships had been lost trying to achieve it. Franklin's expedition was the largest ever mounted.

FRANKLIN'S EXPEDITION

We know that after Franklin sailed past Greenland, he spent his first Arctic winter, of 1845-1846, on Beechey Island. This is where the three sailors' graves were found. His route afterward has been reconstructed from relics left by the sailors, such as tin cans and silver forks, and a single note, written by Franklin's officers, found on King William Island.

The note records that in the summer of 1846, the ships sailed south, only to be trapped by ice off King William Island. Franklin died here, in June 1847, and Captain Crozier took command. In April 1848, after 19 months of being frozen in by ice, Crozier decided to leave the ships, and head south with his men. The last survivors of the Franklin expedition were seen by the local people, the Inuit, in 1850.

ATLANTIC OCEAN
ICELAND
ARCTIC
North Geographic Pole
80° N
30° W
Greenland (to Denmark)
OCEAN
Beechey Island
King William Island
60° W
CANADA
NORTH AMERICA
120° W
90° W

KEY
Permanent pack ice (summer and winter)
Seasonal pack ice (winter)
Franklin's route 1845-1848

▲ ICEBOUND SHIP

This is an artist's impression of one of Franklin's ships, HMS *Terror*, frozen in the ice off King William Island. *Terror* and its sister ship, HMS *Erebus*, were the British Navy's best-equipped vessels. They carried the latest scientific instruments, including a camera, only recently invented. They also carried enough supplies for more than three years, including 8,000 cans of meat, soup, and vegetables.

◄ INUIT STORIES

The Inuit are the only native peoples living in the vast North American Arctic. They are well adapted to living in a freezing climate. According to Inuit stories, in 1850, they saw 40 starving white men walking south over the frozen sea to King William Island. The starving men indicated by signs that their ship had been crushed by the ice. The Inuit later found many of the bodies of these men. Knife marks on the bones showed that the dead had been eaten by their companions.

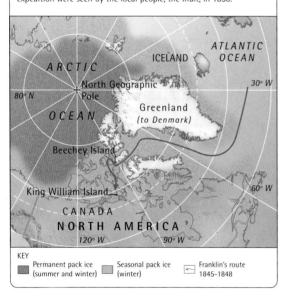

Arctic

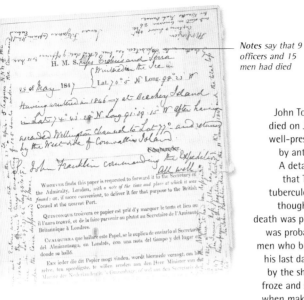

Notes say that 9 officers and 15 men had died

▲ OFFICERS' RECORDS

This is the note written by Franklin's officers and discovered on King William Island. It describes the ships being abandoned in 1848, and also records the deaths of 24 men, including Franklin himself. It does not explain how they had died. This was an unusually high death rate for a well-equipped British expedition. It shows that something had gone terribly wrong.

DEADLY CAN

Franklin was one of the first explorers to use canned food. This can was one of the relics discovered in the Arctic. Many of the cans found were not sealed properly, so the food inside must have rotted. Also, the cans were sealed with lead, which is poisonous. All three dead sailors examined suffered from lead poisoning, which must have caused many of the deaths on the Franklin expedition.

ARCTIC MEMORIAL ▶

From 1848, dozens of expeditions combed the Arctic, searching for Franklin, or trying to learn his fate. The last official expedition, in 1852 to 1854, was led by Captain Edward Belcher, who set up this monument on Beechey Island. Although they never found Franklin, the search parties mapped the entire Canadian Arctic, and found a way through the Northwest Passage.

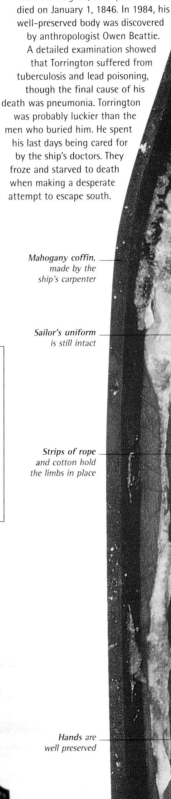

Belcher's monument commemorates all those who died searching for Franklin

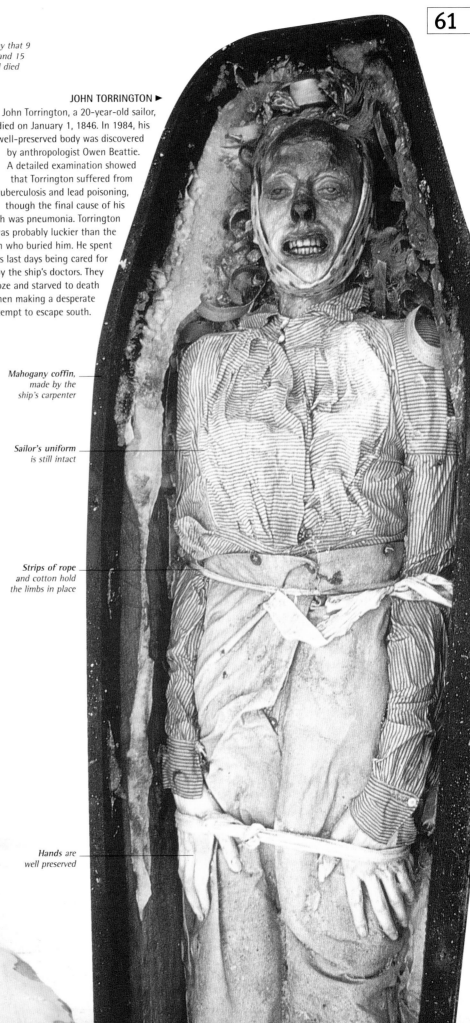

JOHN TORRINGTON ▶

John Torrington, a 20-year-old sailor, died on January 1, 1846. In 1984, his well-preserved body was discovered by anthropologist Owen Beattie. A detailed examination showed that Torrington suffered from tuberculosis and lead poisoning, though the final cause of his death was pneumonia. Torrington was probably luckier than the men who buried him. He spent his last days being cared for by the ship's doctors. They froze and starved to death when making a desperate attempt to escape south.

Mahogany coffin, made by the ship's carpenter

Sailor's uniform is still intact

Strips of rope and cotton hold the limbs in place

Hands are well preserved

OTZI THE ICEMAN

On September 19, 1991, Helmut and Erika Simon, two German hikers in the Ötztal Alps between Austria and Italy, were shocked to find a man's body lying face down in the ice. They assumed he was a modern climber and reported their discovery to the authorities. From the man's strange belongings, including a grass cape and flint-headed arrows, it was soon clear that he was very old indeed. In fact, the dead man, now nicknamed "Ötzi," lived 5,300 years ago, during the Copper Age, when metal tools were first used in Europe.

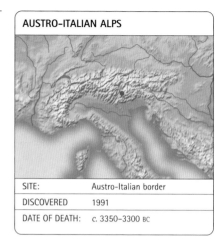

AUSTRO-ITALIAN ALPS

SITE:	Austro-Italian border
DISCOVERED	1991
DATE OF DEATH:	c. 3350–3300 BC

◀ TRAPPED IN ICE
Although Ötzi appeared to be naked when he was found, he was surrounded by fragments of clothes and other belongings. Freeing him from the ice was a difficult process, even with a jackhammer. This photograph was taken on September 20, 1991, when the first attempt to recover him had to be abandoned, because the drill's air supply ran out. Ötzi was not cut free until September 23.

Skin is hairless—the hair has disintegrated

Ice has been drilled away, exposing the body

◀ MAN FROM THE ALPS
Scientists have worked out that Ötzi spent all his life in the Austro-Italian Alpine region. They extracted minerals from his teeth, bones, and intestines, and compared them with water and soil samples taken from a wide area of the Alps. The results suggest that Ötzi was born in a village in the Eisack Valley in Southern Tyrol. He never moved more than 35 miles (60 km) from his birthplace.

Arrowhead

Flint dagger

◀ X-RAY OF A WOUND
The cause of Ötzi's death was discovered in 2001, thanks to this CT scan. It shows a flint arrowhead, between his shoulder blade and his rib cage, that had been fired from behind him. This would have caused severe internal bleeding, which eventually led to his death. The arrow shaft, which Ötzi would have had difficulty pulling out, was missing. This is evidence that he had a companion, who pulled it out for him.

DNA SAMPLING ▲
DNA analysis of blood found in Ötzi's weapons and clothes shows that he died following a fierce fight, involving at least four other people. The blood of two men was found on one arrow blade, suggesting that he had killed two enemies, and then retrieved his arrow. Another man's blood was on his dagger blade. Blood from a fourth man, on Ötzi's clothes, suggests that he had been carrying a wounded companion on his shoulder.

EXAMINING THE BODY ►
Scientists have made a detailed study of Ötzi's body, discovering a great deal about his health. The growth pattern in his one surviving fingernail shows that he had been seriously ill three times in the last year of his life. He suffered from arthritis, too, and was infested with fleas and parasitic worms, which would have given him diarrhea. Scientists also worked out that he was about 46 years old when he died—old age for someone living in prehistoric times.

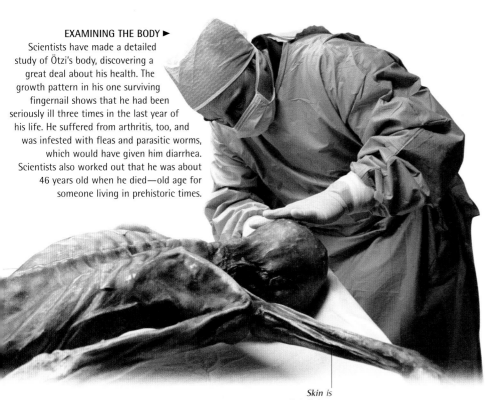

Skin is shriveled up due to dehydration

PRESERVING THE REMAINS ▲
Because Ötzi was found on the Austro-Italian border, there was a dispute about which country he belongs to. At first, he was kept in Austria, at the University of Innsbruck. However, the Italians were able to prove that he had been found 302 ft (92.6 m) within their border, and won him back in 1998. Ötzi can now be seen in his refrigerated viewing chamber, in the specially built South Tyrol Museum of Archaeology, in Bolzano, Italy.

CLOTHING AND EQUIPMENT

BEARSKIN HAT
Ötzi's clothes and belongings—some 70 items—are like a time capsule, showing us life during the Copper Age. His hat, like the soles of his shoes, was made of bearskin. This shows that Ötzi knew how to prepare skins and sew them together, but the absence of woven garments suggests he did not know how to weave cloth.

ARROWS
The deerskin quiver (a case for holding arrows), held 14 arrows made from viburnum and dogwood, with flint blades glued in place with birch tar and tied with sinews. Only two were ready for firing. These had feathers in their shafts, which would have made them spin in flight, improving their accuracy and distance.

COPPER AX
Ötzi's most prized possession was a copper-bladed ax, bound to a yew haft (handle) with leather thongs. He used it to cut and shape wood. Research shows that the copper was mined locally, and one theory is that Ötzi himself was a coppersmith. This is the only complete prehistoric ax ever found.

ÖTZI: RECONSTRUCTED ►
As this reconstruction shows, Ötzi was properly equipped for survival in the Alps. Beneath his grass cape, which could be used as a blanket at night, he wore layers of warm clothing, made from goat and deer hide. He was well armed, with a powerful longbow made from springy yew—the best wood for the purpose. His survival kit included fire-making flints, berries for food, and two lumps of agaric fungus, perhaps as a medicine.

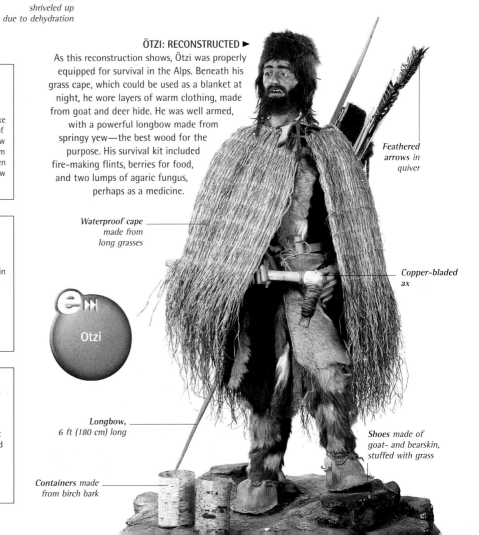

Feathered arrows in quiver

Waterproof cape made from long grasses

Copper-bladed ax

Longbow, 6 ft (180 cm) long

Shoes made of goat- and bearskin, stuffed with grass

Containers made from birch bark

A BOG BODY

On May 8, 1950, two brothers, Emil and Viggo Hoejgaard, were cutting peat near the village of Tollund in Denmark. As they worked, they suddenly saw a face that looked so fresh that they assumed it was that of a recent murder victim. The brothers called the police, who knew of similar finds and summoned the archaeologists. That evening, the leading expert on bog bodies, P. V. Glob, arrived on the scene. From the depth of the peat, Glob knew that the body, now called Tollund Man, was at least 2,000 years old.

bog bodies

▲ THE TOLLUND PEAT BOG
When Tollund Man died, the solid peat in which he was found was a pool of water. It contained tannic acid, a substance that destroys bacteria and preserves skin. To preserve the skin, the water must be cooler than 39°F (4°C) for several months. Like most mummies, Tollund Man probably died in the winter, when the temperature was low. Over time, he was covered by layers of dead vegetation, mostly sphagnum moss, which turned into peat.

NATURALLY PRESERVED ▼
This is the haunting face of Tollund Man. It is remarkably well preserved. He wore a pointed leather cap fastened securely under his chin by a hide thong. There was very short stubble on his chin and upper lip. He looks as if he is at peace, yet the leather noose around his neck indicates that his end was a violent one.

Leather noose drawn around the neck

Leather belt on waist

Day's growth of stubble

▲ THE CAUSE OF DEATH
Tollund Man was found with a leather noose coiled around his neck. The way the noose was placed suggests that Tollund Man had been hanged. After hanging him, his killers had laid him carefully on a thin layer of moss, taking the trouble to close his eyes and place him in a curled-up position, as if asleep.

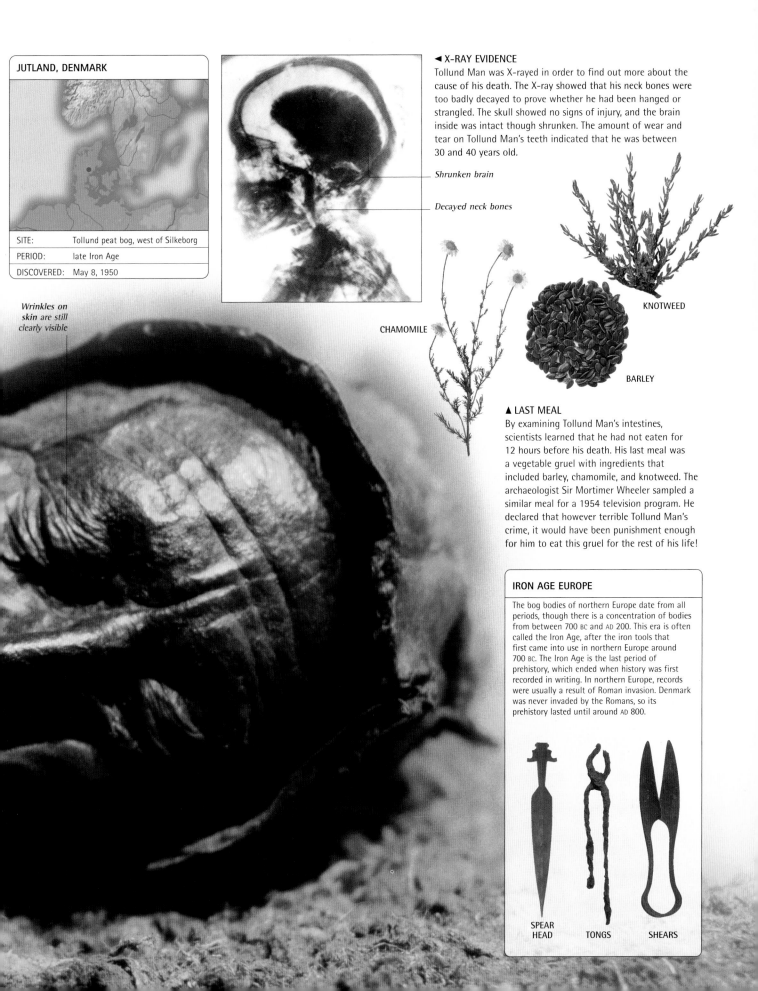

JUTLAND, DENMARK

SITE:	Tollund peat bog, west of Silkeborg
PERIOD:	late Iron Age
DISCOVERED:	May 8, 1950

Wrinkles on skin are still clearly visible

◄ X-RAY EVIDENCE

Tollund Man was X-rayed in order to find out more about the cause of his death. The X-ray showed that his neck bones were too badly decayed to prove whether he had been hanged or strangled. The skull showed no signs of injury, and the brain inside was intact though shrunken. The amount of wear and tear on Tollund Man's teeth indicated that he was between 30 and 40 years old.

Shrunken brain

Decayed neck bones

KNOTWEED

CHAMOMILE

BARLEY

▲ LAST MEAL

By examining Tollund Man's intestines, scientists learned that he had not eaten for 12 hours before his death. His last meal was a vegetable gruel with ingredients that included barley, chamomile, and knotweed. The archaeologist Sir Mortimer Wheeler sampled a similar meal for a 1954 television program. He declared that however terrible Tollund Man's crime, it would have been punishment enough for him to eat this gruel for the rest of his life!

IRON AGE EUROPE

The bog bodies of northern Europe date from all periods, though there is a concentration of bodies from between 700 BC and AD 200. This era is often called the Iron Age, after the iron tools that first came into use in northern Europe around 700 BC. The Iron Age is the last period of prehistory, which ended when history was first recorded in writing. In northern Europe, records were usually a result of Roman invasion. Denmark was never invaded by the Romans, so its prehistory lasted until around AD 800.

SPEAR HEAD   TONGS   SHEARS

BOG SACRIFICES

Well-preserved bodies have been found in bogs across northern Europe for hundreds of years. Yet it is only recently that archaeologists have discovered something remarkable. Where a cause of death can be found, it has always been a violent one. People who died of natural causes were not laid to rest in dark pools. The bog people died from hanging, strangulation, blows to the head, throat-cutting, drowning, and sometimes a combination of methods. Were the bog deaths murders or ritual executions?

WESTERN EUROPE

SITES: 1. Llyn Cerrig Bach, Wales; 2. Lindow Moss, England; 3. Yde, Netherlands; 4. Windeby, Germany; 5. Huldremose, Denmark.

Hollow horn made of sheet bronze

Rivets fasten sheet bronze pieces together

▲ **WATERLOO HELMET**
This bronze helmet was discovered in the Thames River at Waterloo, London, in 1868. Vast quantities of similar metalwork have been found in rivers, lakes, springs, and bogs across northern Europe. Archaeologists do not think it all could have been lost by accident. Objects such as this helmet were too precious to throw away. They must have been deliberately placed in the water, as sacrifices or as offerings to the gods.

Colored glass studs on raised swirls

◄ **BATTERSEA SHIELD**
Like the helmet, this richly decorated bronze shield spent 2,000 years lying at the bottom of the Thames River. It was found at Battersea, London, in 1857. Both pieces show the swirling decoration typical of the Celts, who lived in Britain, Ireland, and other parts of Europe in the Iron Age. The Celts seem to have viewed watery places as sacred entrances to the underworld, the world of the gods.

▲ **LINDOW MAN**
In 1984, peat-diggers at Lindow Moss, near Manchester, England, discovered the 2,000-year-old body of a naked man. Newspapers nicknamed him "Pete Marsh," a pun on the bog he was found in. Examination showed he had been beaten and strangled, had his throat cut, and been dropped face down into the bog. The contents of his stomach revealed that his last meal was a mix of grain, bran, and burned bread. He was between 25 and 30 years old.

bog bodies

YDE GIRL: DISCOVERY, ANALYSIS, AND RECONSTRUCTION

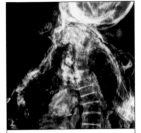

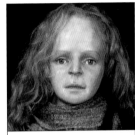

THE REMAINS
In 1897, the body of a teenage girl with long red hair was found in a bog near the Dutch village of Yde. She had been strangled with a 7-ft-long woolen band, which had been wrapped three times around her neck. The Yde Girl was placed on display in the Drent museum at Assen.

DEFORMED SPINE
In the 1980s, scientists studied the Yde Girl and dated her to the 1st century AD. X-rays showed that her wisdom teeth had not developed, and that she was around 16 years old. She also had a stab wound below her collarbone. Her badly curved spine is due to a condition, probably inherited, called scoliosis.

FACIAL RECONSTRUCTION
A CT scan of Yde Girl's head was used to make a plastic model of her skull. Richard Neave, an expert in facial reconstruction, built up her muscles and skin in clay. To do this, he used wooden pegs showing the average thickness of tissues on a teenage girl's face. This is a wax cast of Neave's reconstruction.

DECORATION FOR CHARIOT

BENT SWORD

SLAVE CHAIN

SICKLE

BRIDLE BIT

▲ SACRIFICIAL OBJECTS
In 1943, workers building an airfield on the edge of Llyn Cerrig Bach ("the gravel lake") in Anglesey, Wales, uncovered almost 175 objects. These included chariot fittings, horse bridles, swords, trumpets, cauldrons, and sets of chains used to secure gangs of slaves. These represented repeated offerings, thrown into the lake over a period of 150–200 years. The custom ended in AD 60, when Anglesey was conquered by the Romans.

HULDREMOSE WOMAN ▶
Evidence suggests that at least some of the bog bodies may have been human sacrifices, offered, like the precious metalwork, to gods in watery places. However, we can never be certain why they died. This is the body of Huldremose Woman, another Iron Age body from Denmark. Her well-preserved body showed signs of repeated hacking, and her right arm has been cut off. Whether she was a sacrifice or a murder victim, her death was terrible.

Facial features are well-preserved

Multiple deep wounds indicate repeated hacking

Right arm severed from body

◀ SWORD SACRIFICE
This sword, dating from 1000 BC, was found at Flag Fen in England in the 1980s. It was deliberately damaged before it was thrown into the marsh. Many of the objects found here were similarly broken or bent. This was a way of ritually "killing" them, so that they would be of no further use to the living. They now belonged to the gods who lived beneath the lake. Giving away such precious objects may also have brought prestige to the donors.

▲ WINDEBY GIRL
In 1952, the body of a 14-year-old girl from the 1st century ad was discovered at Windeby in northern Germany. Blindfolded, placed in a pool, and held down by a stone and some birch branches, she probably died from drowning. Like Lindow Man, she belonged to the Germanic peoples, the eastern neighbors of the Celts, who shared many of their customs. Roman writers claimed that the Germans and Celts both practiced human sacrifice.

SAINTS AND RELICS

Followers of Christianity celebrate the lives and works of people known as saints, who are revered for their holiness and special powers. Since the 4th century AD, and possibly before, Christians have preserved bodies and belongings of saints, believing that their powers would remain in these relics. This belief was based on legends about objects that could heal the sick because Christ had touched them. A saint's relic was also a link between humanity on Earth and God in heaven. Pilgrims visited the shrines of saints, where relics lay, to pray for their help in getting to heaven.

HAND OF SAINT JOHN ▲
This gold reliquary (relic holder), from Istanbul, Turkey, is said to contain the right hand of Saint John the Baptist. Using this same hand, John baptized Christ, whom Christians believed to be God in human form. This was, therefore, a highly prized relic that had touched God Himself. Several other shrines have also claimed to own John's right hand, so this relic may not be genuine.

OTHER FAMOUS CATHOLIC SAINTS

Catholic countries preserve the bodies of thousands of saints, with the largest number located in Italy. Below is a list of some of the best-known saints, showing where their remains can be found.

NAME	ROLE	LOCATION OF RELICS
St. James (the Great) (died c. AD 44)	disciple (follower) of Christ	Santiago de Compostela, Spain
St. Peter (died c. AD 64)	disciple of Christ and first pope	Basilica of St. Peter, Rome, Italy
St. Edward the Confessor (1003–1066)	King of England	Westminster Abbey, London, England
St. Francis of Assisi (1181–1226)	founder of the Franciscan Order	Basilica of St. Francis, Assisi, Italy
St. Anthony of Padua (1195–1231)	famous preacher	Basilica of St. Anthony, Padua, Italy
St. Teresa of Avila (1515–1582)	famous nun and visionary	Convent of St. Teresa, Avila, Spain
St. Vincent de Paul (1581–1660)	Franciscan friar	Church of Vincent de Paul, Paris, France
St. Catherine Labouré (1806–1876)	member of the holy order of the Sisters of Charity	Chapel of the Sisters of Charity Convent, Paris, France

◄ STORY OF SAINT MARK
This enamel wall panel, from the Basilica of Saint Mark in Venice, Italy, tells part of an interesting story about relic theft. For any medieval town, the possession of an important saint was a great source of prestige and wealth. The Venetians did not have a saint of their own. So, in AD 828, they stole the body of Saint Mark from Alexandria, Egypt, and brought it to Venice. The thieves claimed to be obeying the saint's own wishes. They said that if he wanted to, he could have used his holy powers to stop them.

INCORRUPTIBLE SAINT ►
Francis Xavier (1506–1552) is a famous example of an "incorruptible," a saint whose body was found to be perfectly preserved after several months in the grave. The Catholic Church regards incorruptibility, or bodily preservation after death, as a clear sign of sainthood. Although most of Francis's natural mummy is now on display in Goa, India, some of his body parts lie elsewhere. The saint's right arm is stored in Rome, Italy, and his inner organs are in various shrines scattered across Asia.

BUDDHIST RELICS

BUDDHIST MONK
This relic is the natural mummy of a Thai Buddhist monk who died in 1973. The religion of Buddhism reveres holy relics, and teaches that they have the power to help the living. The custom of making relics began with the Buddha, the founder of the faith. He asked his followers to preserve his bodily remains after he had passed away.

RELICS OF BUDDHA
There are thousands of relics of the Buddha—such as this one, being carried as part of a procession in Thailand. Buddha was cremated (burned) after death, so most of his relics are tiny fragments of bone and teeth. Buddha's relics are also said to have another power. Buddhists believe that the relics grow in number the more they are venerated.

▲ SAINT BERNADETTE SOUBIROUS
The body of a female saint called Bernadette Soubirous (1844–1879) is another example of incorruptibility. Members of the Church dug up her corpse three times during the early 1900s, to check for signs of decay. A doctor reported that "the body appeared to be absolutely intact." Declared a saint in 1933, she now lies inside a glass case in a shrine in Nevers, France. Her face and hands are covered with a wax coating, made by a company in Paris that normally produced fashion mannequins.

relics

JEWELED RELIQUARY ▶
This gold reliquary, encrusted with precious stones, holds the skull of Saint Foy, a 12-year-old girl who died in Agen, France, in the 4th century AD. In the 9th century, the monks of Conques stole the saint's body from its shrine in Agen, and built this amazing reliquary to contain it. The precious stones were the gifts of pilgrims who wanted to please the saint, for it was said that Saint Foy had a passion for jewelry.

ANNUAL PROCESSION ▶
The festival of Saint Yves is held in Brittany, France, each May. Saint Yves (1253–1303) was a Breton lawyer, famous for his justice and care of the poor. Following his death, he was declared the patron saint of Brittany and of lawyers. During the yearly festival in his honor, leading lawyers carry his skull in a procession from Saint Tugdual Cathedral to the saint's birthplace, the village of Minihy-Tréguier. It is a great honor to be chosen to carry the saint's head.

THE PALERMO MUMMIES

One of the world's largest collections of mummies lies beneath the church of the Capuchin friars in Palermo, Sicily. The oldest mummy dates from 1599, when the friars discovered that the limestone soil beneath their church preserved the bodies buried there. They then made a mummy of a holy friar, called Brother Silvestro, and put him on public display. Soon, the rich citizens of Palermo decided that they wanted to get the same treatment when they died. The catacombs began to fill up with some 8,000 mummified bodies.

THE MUMMIFICATION METHOD

DEHYDRATION
The bodies were left for several months in cells. Here the limestone walls absorbed moisture from the air, drying out the flesh. Then the friars dipped the bodies in baths containing vinegar, arsenic, or lime to help prevent decay.

DRESSED SKELETON
Once dried, the bodies were dressed and put into their chosen place on the walls of the catacombs. The mummies did not last long, though. Over time, their skin and hair gradually crumbled away, eventually leaving skeletons.

▼ **THE CAPUCHIN FRIARS**
This section of the catacombs contains the bodies of Capuchin friars. The holy order of the Capuchin was founded in Italy in the 1520s, with the aim of preaching and caring for the poor. The friars were called Capuchins after their distinctive *cappuccino* (pointed hood). Some of the men shown here may once have played a part in mummifying the Palermo dead.

Hood and habit are light brown, the color of milky coffee

PALERMO, SICILY

SITE:	Church of the Capuchin
PERIOD:	1599–1920
BODY COUNT:	about 8,000 mummies

Palermo

◄ SLEEPING BEAUTY
The only perfectly preserved body in the catacombs is that of Rosalia Lombardo, nicknamed "Sleeping Beauty." Rosalia died in 1920, at the age of two, some 30 years after the friars had stopped making mummies. A local doctor preserved her body by injecting her with certain chemicals, which have not since been identified. He died soon afterward, before he could pass on the secrets of his embalming method.

Many mummies are now little more than skeletons

Skin and hair still survive on this friar

Labels identify each mummy

Lower jaw held in place by wire

Ropes hold mummies in upright position

Some clothes are padded with straw

THE PALERMO CATACOMBS

As members of the Catholic faith, the people of Palermo believed that Christ would eventually return to restore the bodies of the dead to life. In their opinion, there was no better place to await resurrection than inside Palermo's catacombs, where the dead are dressed in their best clothes, ready to be reunited with the loved ones standing around them. During the 18th century, local people made daily trips to these halls to visit their deceased friends and relations. They liked to bring flowers, sit with their loved ones, and perhaps talk to them about their latest news.

▲ ISABELLA GROSSO
The notice inside this display coffin identifies the body as that of a girl named Isabella Grosso who died in the 1870s. By this time, the custom of being mummified for public display was already going out of fashion. Attitudes to death were changing, and many people in Palermo no longer wished to visit the overcrowded catacombs, full of crumbling mummies. By the 1880s, the Sicilian authorities were concerned about the risks to public health and banned the practice of mummification.

THE CORRIDORS OF THE CATACOMBS

SYMBOL OF STATUS
This man wears a top hat, to show people that he was upper-class. Death comes to rich and poor alike, which is why it is often called the "great equalizer." However, the people of Palermo were eager to preserve their social status in death. The halls are divided into sections, depending on gender and social rank.

WOMEN'S FASHION
Knowing that they would be placed in the catacombs following their death, many people left wills describing the clothes they wished to wear while on display. Rich women selected their finest dresses, which they may have worn to church or to a ball. Some of them even carry parasols, as if going on a summertime stroll.

PRIESTS AND PROFESSIONALS
This formally dressed man is from the professionals' hall, one of several male sections. It includes uniformed army officers, university professors, doctors, and lawyers. All of these professional men wear dark, sober suits. In another section, the priests stand on display wearing their colorful, embroidered vestments.

CHILDREN'S DEPARTMENT
The Palermo children have their own section, where lots of small mummies stand in rows, looking down from shelves and niches cut into the limestone walls. Grieving parents may have visited this area to spend time with their departed children, and to be comforted by the thought of being reunited with them in the next life.

CROWDED CORRIDOR ▲
The last part of the catacombs to be built was this corridor, dating from the early 1800s. By this time, there were so many bodies that they had to be stored in coffins that could be stacked on top of one another. Many of these coffins were destroyed on March 11, 1943, during World War II, when the catacombs were hit by bombs.

◄ DIEGO VELASQUEZ
The Capuchin friars claim that one of their mummies belongs to Diego Velasquez (1599–1660), the famous Spanish painter. Although Velasquez visited Italy, he actually died in Spain, and was buried in a church in Madrid. The exact location of his body is no longer known, but it is unlikely to be in Sicily. The rumored presence of Velasquez and several other famous bodies has attracted many visitors to the catacombs. The Palermo mummies are still a tourist attraction today, and the Capuchin friars raise important funds for their order by charging visitors to see them.

Thick, heavy rope around friar's neck

Dehydrated hands hold a prayer book

Body beneath the habit is stuffed with straw

Palermo

PENITENT FRIAR ▲
Several friar mummies inside the catacombs have a thick rope hanging around their neck. In life, the friars wore the rope as a penance—a way of showing God that they were sorry for their sins. By punishing themselves, they hoped to avoid being punished by God after death. As another form of penance, friars would stand inside one of the catacomb niches for hours on end and think about their own death.

MAMMOTH MUMMIES

Elephants now live in the wild in Africa and India, but their ancestors lived on every continent except Antarctica and Australia. The woolly mammoth lived across northern Europe, Asia, and America from 120,000 BC until it became extinct, some 4,000 years ago. Over time, the natural erosion (wearing away) of riverbanks has revealed well preserved mammoths once buried in the frozen soil of Siberia. It is said that the Siberians used to imagine them as giant, molelike beasts that lived and tunneled underground.

Tusks could grow up to 16 ft (5 m) long

WOOLLY MAMMOTHS ▲
Although we use the word "mammoth" to describe something huge, the woolly mammoth was less than 10 ft (3 m) tall at the shoulder, which is actually quite small for an elephant. This smaller body size was an advantage during the Ice Age, when the climate was much colder than it is today, and when food was more scarce. The mammoth was insulated from the cold by a 3-in (90-mm) layer of fat, and by the thick, woolly hair on top, which could grow to 3 ft (90 cm) in length.

mammoths

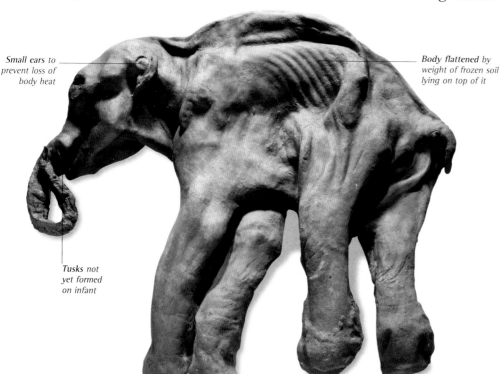

Small ears to prevent loss of body heat

Body flattened by weight of frozen soil lying on top of it

Tusks not yet formed on infant

DIMA ▲
Workers in northeastern Siberia dug up this baby mammoth, nicknamed Dima, in 1977. Dima was a male, between 6 and 12 months of age, and died about 40,000 years ago. Like many frozen mummies, he has lost his coat of hair, making him look more like a modern elephant. We know that he was a woolly mammoth because of his small ears. Modern elephants have developed large ears, which help them to cool down in hot climates.

Internal organs not as well preserved as Dima's

Remains carbon-dated to 40,000 years old

SIBERIA, RUSSIAN FEDERATION

2

1

DISCOVERED: 1977 (Dima), 1988 (Masha)
1. Dima: Magadan region, NE Siberia
2. Masha: Yamal Peninsula, NW Siberia

MASHA ▶
This baby female mammoth, known as Masha, was found in 1988 on the Yamal peninsula, in northwest Siberia. Frozen material along a riverbank had thawed out to expose her body. Eventually, a sailor spotted it when passing by in a boat. Masha, three to four months old, may have died due to an injury to her hind right foot. Unlike Dima, she still has some of her thick, chestnut-colored hair around the feet. Both baby mammoths are now on display in the Zoological Museum in St. Petersburg, Russia.

Woolly coat only partially preserved

MAMMOTH DISCOVERIES

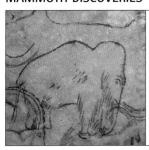

CAVE ART
Cave art, 30,000 years old, shows that mammoths were familiar to our ancestors, who hunted them for meat, fur, and ivory. Prehistoric man even used mammoth remains as a building material on the treeless steppes of Ukraine. Here, archaeologists have found many prehistoric roundhouses, built from mammoth skulls and bones.

DISCOVERY OF DIMA
This photograph shows how Dima appeared when excavators pulled him out of the frozen Siberian soil in 1977. The weight of the earth had flattened the body, and yet the internal organs were very well preserved. DNA was extracted from Dima, which showed that the woolly mammoth was closely related to the Indian elephant.

MAMMOTH DNA
Here, a scientist removes samples of hair and tissue from a woolly mammoth carcass for DNA testing. Some experts believe it may one day be possible to create a living mammoth by injecting the correct DNA into the egg of an Indian elephant. Scientists need to find a complete set of mammoth DNA before they could attempt this.

MAMMOTH GRAVEYARD ▲
Archaeologists in South Dakota have discovered a site containing almost 100 mammoth skeletons. Three of them are of woolly mammoths, and the rest belong to a larger, short-haired species known as the Columbian mammoth. They all died around 26,000 years ago, when they slipped down the edge of a water hole and drowned. The same accident repeated itself over many years, causing this pile-up of bodies.

Tusks are nearly 10 ft (3 m) long

Siberian reindeer sled

TUSK HUNTER ►
Siberian reindeer herders can make extra money by keeping a lookout for mammoth tusks. A famous example of this occurred in 1997, when a nine-year-old Siberian boy named Simeon Jarkov saw the tusk of an adult mammoth sticking out of the snow. He dug both tusks free so that he could sell them. To protect living elephants, it is now illegal to trade their tusks. Mammoths provide the only legal source of tusk ivory, which people carve into decorative objects, or sell (as whole tusks) to collectors and museums.

FROZEN TOMBS

For thousands of years, the vast plains of Asia have been the home of nomadic peoples, who moved from place to place with their animals, searching for fresh pastures. Settled peoples leave behind buildings, but nomads rarely leave any trace that they ever existed. So one of the most important archaeological discoveries of the 20th century was of Siberian tomb mounds, holding the frozen mummies of a nomadic people known as the Pazyryk. It was here, in 1993, that the archaeologist Natalia Polosmak opened the grave of a woman she called the "Ice Maiden."

ASIAN STEPPES

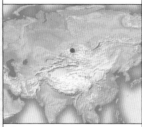

SITE:	Altai mountains
DISCOVERED:	1920s onward
BURIAL DATE:	c. 450 BC–c. 350 BC

EXCAVATION OF FROZEN TOMB ▶
This photograph shows the excavation of the Ice Maiden's tomb. She was buried in the summer, the only time the Siberian soil was not frozen solid. She was placed in a chamber made of larch logs, covered with a mound of earth topped with rocks. Water trickled into the tomb, and froze during the following winter. The mound insulated the burial, preventing the ice inside from thawing, until the mound was dug open 2,400 years later.

◀ ASIAN STEPPES
Steppes—grassy, treeless plains—sweep across a vast region of Asia stretching from the Black Sea to Manchuria. Pazyryk nomads spent most of their lives on the move here, traveling great distances. Yet in the summer they returned to the burial ground in southern Siberia to bury their dead. This must have been a sacred site. It was also one of the few places they could find larch trees, to build their coffins and burial chambers.

Tattoos, made with needles and soot

▲ ARTIFICIALLY PRESERVED
The Pazyryk only buried their dead in the summer when they returned to the burial ground, so they had to find ways to preserve the bodies. Examination of the Ice Maiden showed she had been artificially mummified. Her brain and other organs were removed after death. Her eyes were cut out and the sockets stuffed with fur. The body was filled with bark and peat, which contain a natural preservative called tannin. The Ice Maiden's right thumb, left arm, and left shoulder were covered with tattoos. These show strange creatures resembling deer, which turn into images of flowers and birds.

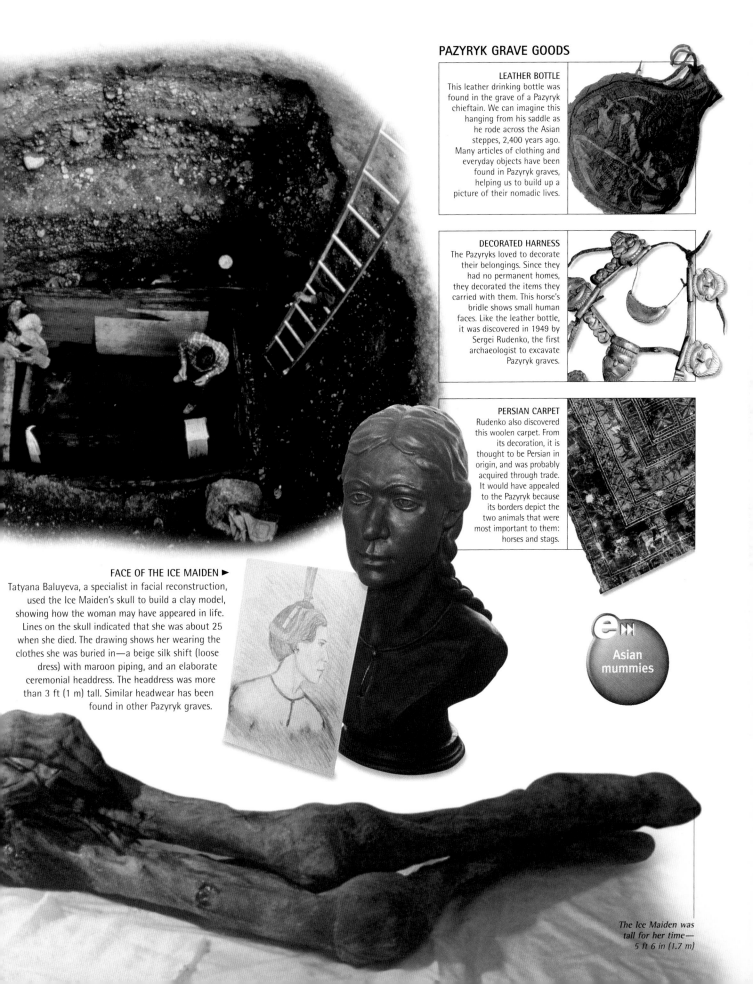

PAZYRYK GRAVE GOODS

LEATHER BOTTLE
This leather drinking bottle was found in the grave of a Pazyryk chieftain. We can imagine this hanging from his saddle as he rode across the Asian steppes, 2,400 years ago. Many articles of clothing and everyday objects have been found in Pazyryk graves, helping us to build up a picture of their nomadic lives.

DECORATED HARNESS
The Pazyryks loved to decorate their belongings. Since they had no permanent homes, they decorated the items they carried with them. This horse's bridle shows small human faces. Like the leather bottle, it was discovered in 1949 by Sergei Rudenko, the first archaeologist to excavate Pazyryk graves.

PERSIAN CARPET
Rudenko also discovered this woolen carpet. From its decoration, it is thought to be Persian in origin, and was probably acquired through trade. It would have appealed to the Pazyryk because its borders depict the two animals that were most important to them: horses and stags.

FACE OF THE ICE MAIDEN ▶
Tatyana Baluyeva, a specialist in facial reconstruction, used the Ice Maiden's skull to build a clay model, showing how the woman may have appeared in life. Lines on the skull indicated that she was about 25 when she died. The drawing shows her wearing the clothes she was buried in—a beige silk shift (loose dress) with maroon piping, and an elaborate ceremonial headdress. The headdress was more than 3 ft (1 m) tall. Similar headwear has been found in other Pazyryk graves.

Asian mummies

The Ice Maiden was tall for her time— 5 ft 6 in (1.7 m)

HORSE MUMMIES

For many thousands of years, wild horses roamed across Europe and Asia. They appear in prehistoric cave paintings from 30000 BC, when people hunted them for meat. Horses were later captured from the wild and kept for meat and milk. Then, at some time before 2000 BC, people on the Asian steppes made a discovery that would change human history. They learned to ride horses and use them to pull loads. Horseback riding made nomadic life possible. Horses were so important to the Pazyryk nomads that they even buried them with their dead.

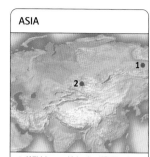

ASIA

1. Wild horse: Yakutia, NE Siberia
2. Pazyryk horse: Altai mountains, S. Siberia

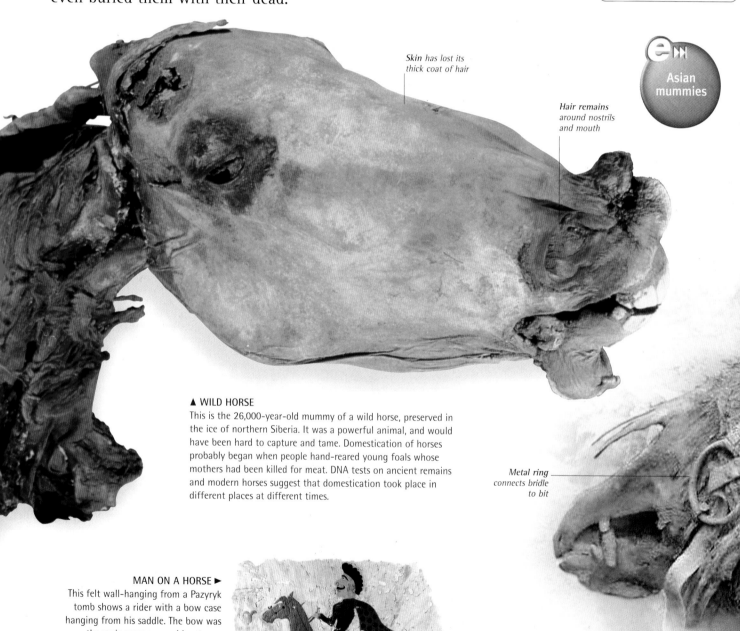

Skin has lost its thick coat of hair

Hair remains around nostrils and mouth

Asian mummies

Metal ring connects bridle to bit

▲ WILD HORSE
This is the 26,000-year-old mummy of a wild horse, preserved in the ice of northern Siberia. It was a powerful animal, and would have been hard to capture and tame. Domestication of horses probably began when people hand-reared young foals whose mothers had been killed for meat. DNA tests on ancient remains and modern horses suggest that domestication took place in different places at different times.

MAN ON A HORSE ▶
This felt wall-hanging from a Pazyryk tomb shows a rider with a bow case hanging from his saddle. The bow was the main weapon used by steppe nomads. Because the nomads could ride horses, they were able to travel vast distances across the steppes, in search of new pastures for their flocks of sheep and cattle. The power and speed of a horse also made them great hunters and fighters.

BRIDLED HORSE ▲
The invention of the bridle helped people control their horses. This well-preserved horse's head and bridle was found in a Pazyryk grave mound buried with its owner. The bridle consists of leather strips fitted over the animal's head, with a metal bar, called a bit, passing through the animal's mouth. The bridle is connected to reins. By pulling on the reins, people could make the horse change direction.

◄ SCYTHIAN COIN
The nomads to the north of the Black Sea were known to the ancient Greeks as the Scythians. This Scythian coin, in Greek style, shows a mounted warrior with a spear. It is hard for us to imagine the impact of seeing a man riding a horse for the first time. Perhaps it inspired the Greek legends about centaurs—creatures that were half human and half horse.

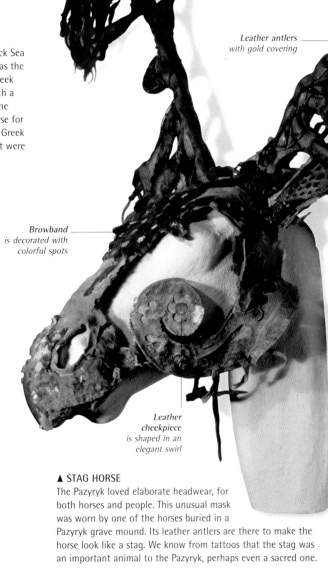

Leather antlers
with gold covering

Browband
is decorated with
colorful spots

Leather
cheekpiece
is shaped in an
elegant swirl

Horses and riders
rest under a tree

SADDLES AND BRIDLES ▲
This silver belt buckle comes from a steppe nomad's grave and is good evidence for early tack (riding equipment), such as bridles and saddles. The saddles have two girths (leather strips used to attach the saddle to the horse) that are loose here. The saddles have no stirrups. The stirrup, which helps make a rider stable on a horse, was not invented until after AD 200.

▲ STAG HORSE
The Pazyryk loved elaborate headwear, for both horses and people. This unusual mask was worn by one of the horses buried in a Pazyryk grave mound. Its leather antlers are there to make the horse look like a stag. We know from tattoos that the stag was an important animal to the Pazyryk, perhaps even a sacred one.

Leather bridle
is still around
head

NOMADIC PEOPLES ▲
Nomadic peoples still live on the Asian steppes, preserving customs that go back thousands of years. Many are still accomplished horse riders, and they learn to ride at a very early age. The nomadic farmers move with their herds of sheep, goats, and cattle from the summertime pastures in the mountains to the grassy lowland steppes during the winter. They also take part in ancient riding competitions and games, which the Pazyryk may have played more than 2,000 years ago.

DESERT DISCOVERIES

Since the 1970s, Chinese archaeologists have discovered about 100 well-preserved mummies on the edges of the Takla Makan Desert in northwest China. These mummies are known by several names, including the Cherchen, Tarim Basin, Takla Makan, and Ürümchi, depending on the place where they were found or are now kept. Unexpectedly, they have the features of white Europeans rather than Asians. They have light hair and long noses, and the men have full beards. The mummies date from 2000 to 1000 BC. How people related to Europeans came to be living in what is now China at such an · early date is a mystery.

BEAUTY OF LOULAN ▶

This female mummy was discovered in 1980 by the Chinese archaeologist Mu Shun Ying. He nicknamed her the "Beauty of Loulan," after the place where she was found. Over her long brown hair, she wears a felt hat trimmed with a goose feather. She was buried with a bag of wheat and a tray used for winnowing (separating grains from husks). Both these items suggest she was a farmer. She has been carbon-dated to 1800 BC.

◀ TAKLA MAKAN DESERT

The name "Takla Makan" is said to mean "go in and you won't come out." One of the harshest places on Earth, this is also a perfect environment for preserving bodies. Those buried in winter were prevented from decomposing by temperatures well below freezing. By the time the heat of summer arrived, the large amount of salt in the soil had dried them out, producing natural mummies.

Winnowing tray was found under the body

Woolen cape is still tightly wrapped around body

Bag of wheat lay in the grave

TAKLA MAKAN DESERT, CHINA

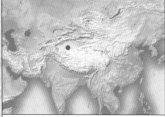

SITE:	Takla Makan Desert
PERIOD:	2000 BC–1000 BC
BODY COUNT:	about 100 so far

 Asian mummies

Shoes made from leather

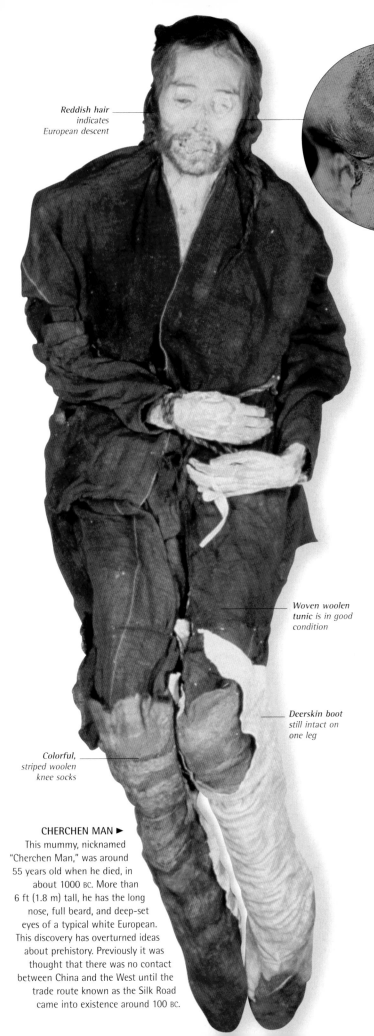

SUN SYMBOL TATTOO
The left temple of Cherchen Man was painted with a yellow ocher image of a sun disc, with shining rays. This may have been a religious symbol. Many of the graves were laid out in an east–west direction, which suggests that the rising and setting of the sun was important to the Takla Makan people. The graves at the Loulan site were surrounded by great circles of logs, perhaps another sun symbol.

SIGNS OF AGRICULTURE ►
The discovery of farming equipment and animal remains, such as this goat's skull, suggests that the people of the Takla Makan were farmers. They lived in villages around the edge of the desert. Here they could grow wheat and raise animals, including goats and sheep for food and leather, and donkeys for transportation. They were also skilled weavers who knew how to make felt for blankets and hats from wool.

Wooden stake runs through goat's skull

TAKLA MAKAN CRAFTS

NOMADIC SHEPHERDS
The Takla Makan people probably traded with nomadic shepherds to get wool. Like today's Mongolian herders, shepherds would have spent their lives on the move, crossing the wide grasslands north of the desert. The Takla Makan people did not have enough pasture for sheep to produce fine wool.

BABY BEAKER
The people of the Takla Makan even found use for sheep udders—this baby's drinking cup was made from one. Everyday items like this help us reconstruct the lives of Takla Makan people, which seem to have been peaceful. Except for a few bows and arrows for hunting, no weapons have been found.

WOVEN FABRIC
Examination of the mummies' woven textiles shows that they are similar to fabrics produced in Europe before 500 BC. The people of the Takla Makan used plants and minerals to produce a range of bright dyes, and wove their wool into patterns including plaids, stripes, and checks.

Reddish hair indicates European descent

Woven woolen tunic is in good condition

Deerskin boot still intact on one leg

Colorful, striped woolen knee socks

CHERCHEN MAN ►
This mummy, nicknamed "Cherchen Man," was around 55 years old when he died, in about 1000 BC. More than 6 ft (1.8 m) tall, he has the long nose, full beard, and deep-set eyes of a typical white European. This discovery has overturned ideas about prehistory. Previously it was thought that there was no contact between China and the West until the trade route known as the Silk Road came into existence around 100 BC.

CHINESE TOMBS

Like the Egyptians, the ancient Chinese regarded a tomb as a home for a dead person who would live again. They built palacelike underground tombs with luxurious rooms, full of precious possessions, where their rulers could exist in the afterlife. The tombs even had their own servants and soldiers, represented by terra-cotta or wooden figures. The Chinese also attempted to preserve bodies by encasing them in jade, or by placing them in sealed coffins. In some cases, they filled the sealed coffins with a special embalming fluid.

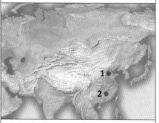

IMPERIAL CHINA

1. Tomb of Princess Tou Wan: Mancheng, Hebei Province

2. Tomb of Lady Dai: Changsha

TERRA-COTTA ARMY ▲

The tomb of Quin Shi Huangdi, China's first emperor and founder of the Quin dynasty, is so large that archaeologists have not yet finished excavating it. He was buried, in 210 BC, with an army of more than 7,000 terra-cotta soldiers to protect him in the afterlife. In 1974, about 1.2 miles (2 km) from the emperor's vast tomb mound, a group of peasants unearthed fragments of one of these life-size warriors. The most famous Chinese tombs all date from between 221 BC and AD 9, when the country was ruled by the Quin and Han dynasties.

◄ BRONZE LAMP

This gilded bronze oil lamp was one of hundreds of precious grave goods found in the tomb of Tou Wan, a princess of the Han dynasty. Whoever made this lamp also designed it to be a servant girl to the princess in the afterlife. About 19 in (48 cm) high, it has sliding panels to control the brightness and direction of the light.

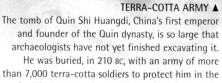

Ancient China

▼ JADE BURIAL SUIT

Tou Wan was the wife of a local ruler, Liu Sheng, who was the son of the Han emperor. When she died, her body was placed inside this suit, made up of small squares of jade sewn together with gold thread. The Chinese valued jade for its beautiful color and hardness. Because it does not perish, jade was also a symbol of eternal life for the Chinese. The jade lasted, but the body inside decayed.

Suit made up of 2,156 individual pieces of jade

Nephrite was the exact type of jade used

Entire suit such as this would take a modern jadesmith about 10 years to complete

Gilded pillow, inlaid with jade

Crow standing in front of the sun—also related to Chinese legends of immortality

Toad on a crescent moon, connected with legends of immortality

LADY DAI'S MUMMY ▼
The body of Lady Dai, who died in around 180 BC, lay inside three nested coffins in a wooden tomb chamber. The walls of the chamber were sealed with layers of charcoal and white clay, which kept out oxygen and moisture. These conditions preserved her so well that her body, when found, was like that of someone who had recently died. Two other well preserved Han dynasty mummies have also been found, inside coffins filled with an unidentified embalming liquid.

Dragons, seen as protective creatures

Hair still intact

Gatekeepers guarding entrance to Heaven

FUNERARY BANNER ▶
This beautiful painted silk banner was placed over the coffin of a Chinese noblewoman, from the Han dynasty, called Lady Dai. The scenes depict her journey to immortality. The wider area at the top represents the heavens, inhabited by gods, dragons, immortals, and sacred animals. Lower down, the banner shows Lady Dai traveling from Earth up toward the heavens, accompanied by three servants. Two gatekeepers protect the entrance to the heavens.

Body was 50 years old at time of death, c. 168 BC

Lady Dai with her servants

Wiry gold thread used to sew jade pieces together, as a sign of royal status

▲ LADY DAI'S TOMB
Lady Dai's tomb lay inside a hill called Mawangdui on the outskirts of the modern city of Changsha, in the Yangtse Valley. Archaeologists discovered the tomb in 1971, while investigating a site where a new hospital was about to be built. As well as the body and the banner, the tomb chamber contained more than 1,000 treasures, including lacquer bowls, food, medicinal herbs, and more than 100 wooden figures.

Underworld, where a giant supports weight of Earth

SELF-MADE MUMMIES

In the mountains of northern Japan there is a group of mummies unlike any others. They were self-made by men who chose to mummify themselves while they were still alive. The men were priests belonging to a religious group called Shingon Buddhism, which practiced self-denial. Self-denial was a way of training the mind to ignore the physical world and concentrate on spirituality. These priests hoped to leave their mummies behind as a symbol of great holiness, to inspire Buddhists who lived after them.

YAMAGATA MOUNTAINS, JAPAN

REGION:	Yamagata Province
PERIOD:	14th century onward
BODY COUNT:	between 16 and 24 (estimate)

Buddhist mummies

◄ MUMMY ON DISPLAY ►
This is the mummy of Shinyokai, a priest who died at the age of 95 in 1788. Buddhists believe that after death we are reborn in new bodies. The goal of Buddhism is to escape from this cycle of death and rebirth, by achieving a sacred state called enlightenment. Becoming a self-made mummy was believed to be a sign that a Buddhist priest had reached enlightenment. Like other self-made mummies, Shinyokai is dressed in rich robes and displayed in a Buddhist temple, where he is worshiped as a god.

String of 112 wooden beads was used in prayer

CHUKAI ▶

A self-made mummy was called a *shokushinbutsu*, meaning "Buddha of the body." This is the *shokushinbutsu* of Chukai (1697–1755). Like other Shingon monks, he spent years training his body to ignore pain before mummifying himself. One way of doing this was to sit in a room filled with smoke from burning peppers.

TETSUMONKAI ▶

This is the *shokushinbutsu* of Tetsumonkai, who died in 1829. He is kept in the Churenji temple in the Yamagata Province. Legend has it that he became a Buddhist monk after killing two Samurai warriors in self-defense. He practiced self-denial in remorse for his actions. One of his self-punishments was to sit in the lotus position (cross-legged, with feet on top of his thighs) beneath an icy waterfall.

◀ KUKAI

This is a statue of Kukai (AD 774–835), the Buddhist monk who introduced Shingon Buddhism to Japan. After studying different forms of Buddhism in China in the early 800s, he set up a monastery in Japan. This practiced a new type of Buddhism. Most Buddhists believe that it takes many lifetimes to achieve enlightenment. Kukai thought it was possible to attain enlightenment in one lifetime, through self-denial and self-mummification.

KAIKOJI TEMPLE ▶

The Kaikoji temple in Sakata holds the mummies of Chukai (1697–1755) and Enyokai (1767–1822). They have been cared for by generations of Buddhist priests. Local people still regard these mummies as gods. Today more than 10 million Japanese people—a tenth of the country's Buddhists— follow Shingon Buddhism. But self-mummification has been illegal since the late 19th century.

STEPS TO SELF-MUMMIFICATION

A SPECIAL DIET
Kukai's method of self-mummification was a long and painful process that took about ten years. The first step was to change the diet, in order to lose body fat. The priests gave up eating their usual food of rice and wheat, and ate pine kernels, bark, and roots instead.

URUSHI TEA
Next, the priests drank tea made from the sap of the Urushi tree, which was normally used to make varnish for furniture. The tea was poisonous, and made the priests vomit and sweat, which dehydrated their bodies. They believed that it would help to preserve their bodies after death.

ARSENIC
Toward the end of the mummification process, the priests probably drank water from a sacred spring. Recently, scientists discovered that water from this spring contains arsenic. Arsenic is a poison that builds up in body tissues. It would have killed any bacteria inside a body that normally causes it to decay after death.

WALLED UP
In the last stage, the priest was walled up in a tiny cell for 1,000 days. The inside of the cell received air through a tube. The priest rang a bell each day to show that he was still alive. When the ringing ceased, the tube was blocked up. After 1,000 days, the priest's followers opened the cell to see if the process had worked.

MODERN-DAY MUMMIES

Since the late 19th century, the funeral industry has developed new methods for preserving the dead. Embalmers inject bodies with preservatives so that they can be displayed to friends and relatives at funerals. Some famous political leaders have also been permanently embalmed for public show. Another form of modern preservation is cryonics. Named after the Greek word *kryos* ("icy cold"), cryonics involves chilling a body soon after death. People who sign up for this procedure hope that scientists will one day have the technology to bring them back to life.

▲ LENIN

The most famous modern mummy is that of Vladimir Lenin (1870–1924), founder of the Soviet Union. After his death, specially chosen scientists removed his organs, injected his body with embalming fluids, and soaked the entire corpse in a bath of preservatives. The method was not perfect, and Lenin now needs constant attention to ensure his continued preservation. Every 18 months, his body is removed from display to be re-soaked in a vat of embalming fluid.

EMBALMING: THE HOLMES METHOD

Dr. Thomas Holmes (1817–1900) is known as "the father of modern embalming." He was an officer in the US Army Medical Corps during the Civil War (1861–65). Holmes invented a method of preserving dead soldiers, so that they could be sent home for burial. He injected embalming fluid, containing arsenic, into the arteries, using a pump to make it circulate throughout the body.

By the end of the war, Holmes claimed to have embalmed 4,028 men. Almost all were officers, whose families could afford to pay the $100 fee Holmes charged. A side effect of Holmes's method is that many US 19th-century cemeteries are now contaminated with high levels of poisonous arsenic. Embalmers still use this technique, but they now inject a safer chemical, called formaldehyde, discovered in 1868.

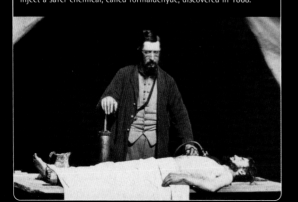

▲ LENIN'S TOMB

Lenin's mummy was placed in a mausoleum in Moscow's Red Square by order of his political successor, Joseph Stalin. Stalin believed that the Soviet people needed a figure to worship. Although the Soviet Union broke up in 1991, Lenin remains in the mausoleum, and tourists still line up to see him. In 2004, an opinion poll revealed that 56 percent of Russians believe he should be removed from display and properly buried.

FROM SURGERY TO COLD STORAGE

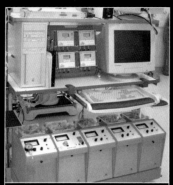

SURGERY
Cryonics patients can choose from two services—preserving the whole body, for about $120,000, or the head alone, which costs about $50,000. Both services require major surgery as soon as possible after death. For the complete service, a team of surgeons must open the patient's chest to reach the arteries.

CRYOPROTECTANTS
Once they have reached the arteries, the surgeons pump all the blood out of the body and replace it with "cryoprotectant solution," designed to minimize tissue damage. This process takes four hours. Similar methods are used to preserve heads. It is claimed that, in the future, it will be possible to regrow a new body for each preserved head.

NITROGEN
Cryonics surgeons use nitrogen vapor to cool the body or head gradually over a period of two weeks, until it reaches a temperature of –321°F (–196°C). Then they place the body or head inside a steel cylinder filled with liquid nitrogen, which is replaced every few weeks. This is not true freezing but "vitrification," an ice-free preservation process.

VACUUM FLASKS
Each large steel cylinder can hold four bodies, stored upright. Smaller cylinders are used to store individual heads. Like vacuum flasks, the steel cylinders have double walls for insulation. Even if the bodies cannot be revived, the cryonics process is creating hundreds of perfectly preserved mummies for future surgeons and scientists to study.

e⋙ modern mummies

▼ IDENTITY TAGS

Human cells begin to break down quickly after death, so cryonics patients need to ensure that they are chilled as soon as possible. They wear medical alert bracelets and neck tags, which give the telephone number to be called in the event of their sudden death. These tags also give special instructions to doctors or paramedics: "If Dead Cool with Ice Especially Head. Do Not Embalm or Autopsy." A reward is offered for following the instructions correctly.

IDENTITY NECKLACE

IDENTITY BRACELET

CRYONICS IN THE MOVIES

Preservation by cryonics was first suggested by Robert C. W. Ettinger in his 1964 book *The Prospect of Immortality*. Ettinger argued, "No matter what kills us... sooner or later our friends of the future should be equal to the task of reviving and curing us." Many have disagreed. The people of the future, living on a planet with a soaring population, might not wish to revive the dead. Also, the revived might have difficulty adjusting to a world in which everything and everyone was unfamiliar.

Cryonics has inspired a number of movies, including Steve Miner's *Forever Young* (1992). In this film, Mel Gibson plays a 1939 test pilot, called Daniel McCormick, who volunteers to be frozen for a year as part of an army medical experiment. The experiment goes wrong, and McCormick wakes up in 1992, 53 years into the future.

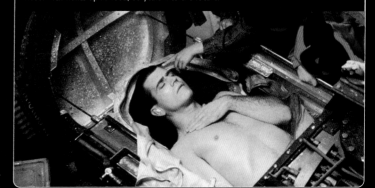

▲ CRYONIC SUSPENSION

The Alcor Life Extension Foundation in Scottsdale, Arizona, is the leading company offering "cryonic suspension." At Alcor's headquarters, the chilled dead are stored in steel cylinders such as these. The aim is to preserve the brain and body, so that doctors can revive them in the future. For this to happen, medical science will have to move on greatly. In 2004, there were 59 people inside Alcor's cylinders, and 650 living clients waiting to be preserved.

MUMMIES ON DISPLAY

In the 19th century, large audiences paid to watch Egyptian mummies being unwrapped. This fascination with the preserved dead has continued through to the 21st century. Today, Ötzi the Iceman, Juanita the Ice Maiden, and numerous other mummies are on display in museums all over the world, where they are the star attractions. New mummies are also being created specifically for public display, both as objects of art and in order to teach people about human and animal anatomy.

FOR ART ▶

Damien Hirst (b. 1965) is a British artist who often preserves dead animals as part of his work. Through his art, Hirst tries to make us examine our attitude toward death. He also wants us to think about the relationships between people and animals, and between art and life. In 1994, he put this lamb in a glass case filled with formaldehyde. Its title, *Away from the Flock*, draws our attention to the lamb's state of isolation and vulnerability.

Lacerta

2222

▲ FOR SCIENCE
Medical collections often include preserved people and animals. The Wellcome Museum of Medical Science was founded in 1914 by Henry Solomon Wellcome (1853–1936), a rich American fascinated by the history of medicine. He used his wealth to build up a vast collection, including unusually deformed animals, such as this lizard born with two tails. The museum closed in 1985, when its collection was transferred to London's Science Museum.

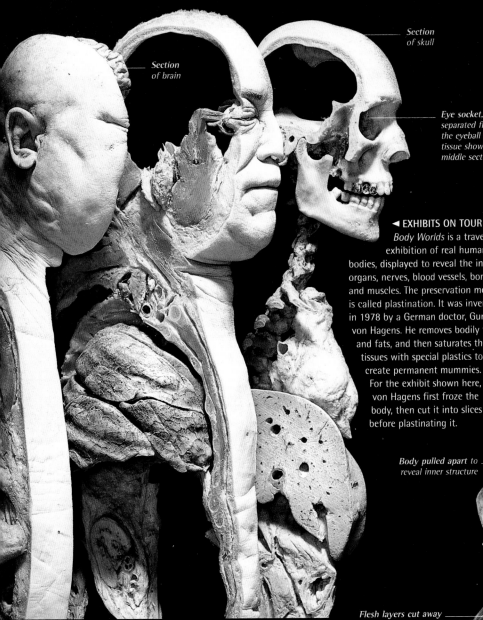

Section of brain

Section of skull

Eye socket, separated from the eyeball and tissue shown in middle section

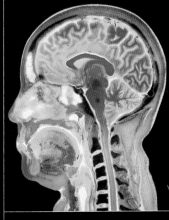

◄ EXHIBITS ON TOUR

Body Worlds is a traveling exhibition of real human bodies, displayed to reveal the inner organs, nerves, blood vessels, bones, and muscles. The preservation method is called plastination. It was invented in 1978 by a German doctor, Gunther von Hagens. He removes bodily fluids and fats, and then saturates the tissues with special plastics to create permanent mummies. For the exhibit shown here, von Hagens first froze the body, then cut it into slices before plastinating it.

WILLING EXHIBITS

The people on display in the *Body Worlds* exhibition, such as the man whose head appears here, all requested it in their wills. Von Hagens also wants his body to be plastinated and displayed when he dies. He sees plastination as an opportunity to "put yourself in the next generation as an example of human construction."

Body pulled apart to reveal inner structure

Flesh layers cut away to expose muscles and organs beneath

JEREMY BENTHAM ►

The English philosopher Jeremy Bentham (1748–1832) asked a surgeon friend to preserve his body after death and put it on display "to save his friends the expense of commissioning a sculpture." His skeleton is still on display at University College London, dressed in his own clothes and seated in the posture he liked to adopt when thinking deeply. The head on display is made of wax. Bentham's mummified head, shown between his feet here, is usually kept locked up.

display

▲ CONTROVERSIAL EXHIBITS

One of the displays in *Body Worlds* is of a man riding a horse and looking down at his own brain, which he holds in his right hand. By arranging such striking poses, von Hagens hopes to entertain as well as educate the public. Some critics have accused him of poor taste. But von Hagens says that his aim is to help visitors to "understand themselves as a piece of wonderful nature."

MUMMY TIMELINE

Dead bodies have been naturally and artificially mummified for thousands of years. This timeline shows you who was mummified when, and how. It also gives details of significant discoveries and archaeological excavations related to mummies.

timelines

c. 5000 BC A fishing tribe called the Chinchorro, living on the northern coast of what is now modern Chile, begin to embalm their dead.

c. 4000 BC The Paloma people of Peru are mummifying their dead using salt to stop decay. They wrap the mummies in reed matting and bury them under the floors of their homes.

c. 3350–3300 BC A European man, whom archaeologists later call "Ötzi the Iceman," freezes to death in the Alps. His body is frozen in a glacier.

c. 3200 BC The oldest surviving Egyptian mummies are buried in the desert sand, where they are naturally dried and mummified.

2686–2160 BC During the Old Kingdom in ancient Egypt, mummies of kings and queens are buried in pyramids.

2589 BC Pharaoh Khufu commissions the Great Pyramid, the largest of the ancient Egyptian tombs. It was built in Giza, on the west bank of the Nile River, and finished in c. 2550 BC.

c. 2000 BC The ancient Egyptians start to embalm some of the body's internal organs separately. They store the organs in canopic jars.

1492 BC Death of Pharaoh Thutmose I. He is the first pharaoh to have his tomb built in the Valley of the Kings, west of the Nile in Egypt.

1327 BC Death of the 17-year-old pharaoh Tutankhamun. He is buried inside a small tomb in the Valley of the Kings.

c. 1000 BC Egyptian priests rescue a number of royal mummies from tombs in the Valley of the Kings that have been disturbed by robbers. They rebury them in secret hiding places.

c. 500 BC People on the Paracas Peninsula in Peru preserve their dead by wrapping them in bundles and burying them in the desert.

450 BC The Greek historian Herodotus visits Egypt and writes down one of the first eyewitness accounts of the mummification process.

c. AD 50–100 A man is killed, perhaps as a religious sacrifice, in Cheshire, England. His corpse is thrown into the Lindow Moss bog, where it is preserved.

AD 79 Mount Vesuvius in Italy erupts, burying the towns of Pompeii and Herculaneum under rock and ash. The ash forms a hard crust around the bodies of the victims, and makes a mold of their bodies.

800s The Chachapoya (Cloud People) of northern Peru begin to mummify their dead. Their civilization is conquered by the Incas in about AD 1475.

835 The Buddhist priest Kukai dies after a period of self-mummification that involves gradual, deliberate starvation.

1000s The Chimu people of northern Peru mummify their dead and bury them in textile bundles.

1100 The Incas begin to rule along the Andes Mountains, from modern-day Ecuador to Chile and Bolivia. Sacrificial children are buried in the mountains, where the bodies are freeze-dried by the cold. The Inca empire lasts until the 1530s.

c. 1475 Eight Inuit people are mummified by dry air and freezing temperatures in Greenland.

1552 St. Francis Xavier dies on the Chinese island of Sancian. Several months after his death, his body is exhumed (dug up) and found to be intact.

1599 Friars in Palermo, Sicily, mummify the dead body of Brother Silvestro from Gubbio. His remains are placed on display in the church's catacombs.

1792 Johann Blumenbach, a German physician and anthropologist, unwraps dozens of mummies across England. Large audiences pay to watch the unrollings.

1798 Napoleon Bonaparte invades Egypt. French scholars remove mummy cases from tombs for study in Paris.

1800s In Japan, Buddhist priests are mummified using a smoking process.

1832 The head of British philosopher Jeremy Bentham is mummified. Then his head and body are dressed and placed in a sitting pose.

1845 British explorer Sir John Franklin leads an expedition in the Arctic to find the Northwest Passage. Franklin and his men never return.

1852 In Great Britain, mummy collector Thomas Pettigrew mummifies the dead Duke of Hamilton at the duke's request. The duke even has an ancient Egyptian stone sarcophagus to house his body.

1868 The German chemist August Wilhelm von Hofman discovers formaldehyde. Its preservative properties become the foundation for modern methods of embalming.

1875 Archaeologists uncover a huge, ancient burial site in Ancón, Peru. Deep shafts lead to tombs where hundreds of well-preserved mummy bundles are found. The mummies are wrapped in cloth, seaweed, leaves, grass matting, and furs. Many bundles have a false head, decorated with eyes that stare out into the darkness of the tomb.

1879 St. Bernadette dies. She is exhumed by the Catholic Church several times in the early 1900s. Each time, her body is found to be well preserved.

1880s Authorities in Palermo ban the practice of mummification.

1881 A cache of royal mummies is discovered in Deir el-Bahri, near the Valley of the Kings in Egypt. It contains more than 50 mummies of kings, queens, and courtiers. Among them are Rameses II and his father, Seti I.

1896 Remains are exhumed in a cemetery in Guanajuato, Mexico, to make room for the recently deceased. To the amazement of the authorities, they find the corpses have been mummified naturally.

1897 The preserved body of a teenage girl, later known as "Yde Girl," is found in a bog near Yde in the Netherlands.

1898 A second cache of mummies is discovered in the Valley of the Kings. The tomb of Amenhotep II is found to contain 16 mummies, 10 of them royal.

1917 German archaeologist Max Uhle discovers the world's oldest artificially preserved corpses. They are the remains of the Chinchorro from South America.

1920 In Palermo, a doctor embalms the body of Rosalia Lombardo using chemicals. Nicknamed "Sleeping Beauty," Rosalia's mummy is one of the last to be installed in the Palermo catacombs, Sicily.

1920s The oldest known Peruvian mummies are found on the peninsula of Paracas in Peru. Almost all of the 429 mummies found there are the remains of elderly men.

1921 Dr. Paul Nordlung recovers a number of frozen remains from the Jerjolfs-nes graveyard in Greenland. Dating from around AD 1000, they are the remains of Viking settlers.

1922 Archaeologist Howard Carter opens up the undisturbed tomb of Tutankhamun in the Valley of the Kings in Egypt. Over several years, Carter retrieves Tutankhamun's mummy and a vast quantity of royal treasure.

1924 Russian revolutionary leader Vladimir Lenin dies. His body is preserved using chemicals and is put on permanent display in Red Square, Moscow.

1949 American chemist Willard Libby comes up with the idea of using Carbon 14 to determine the age of organic (plant or animal) remains. This method becomes known as radiocarbon dating.

1950 The 2,000-year-old preserved body of a man is discovered in the Tollund bog in Denmark. The man later becomes known as "Tollund Man."

1952 Eva Perón, wife of the leader of Argentina, dies. Her embalmers spend a year carefully removing her bodily fluids and replacing them with paraffin wax.

A 14-year-old girl, who dates from the 1st century AD, is found in a bog in Windeby, northern Germany.

1962 Physics professor Robert Ettinger proposes the idea of cryonic suspension in his book *The Prospect of Immortality* (published for the commercial market in 1964). He argues that if personality and identity are simply properties of the brain's structure, then preserving the brain should preserve individuals.

1967 By his own request, American psychology professor Dr. James Bedford becomes the first human to be placed in cryonic suspension. He remains in a chilled state, in the hope that one day medical science will be able to bring him back to life and cure the cancer that killed him.

1970s The treasures of King Tutankhamun go on tour all around the world. Between 1976 and 1978, the treasures tour the United States and attract about 8 million visitors.

Perfectly preserved 3,000-year-old mummies begin to be found in the Takla Makan Desert in China. The bodies are unrelated to modern Chinese people, and have European features such as reddish-blond hair and long noses. They are believed to be members of an ancient nomadic civilization.

1971 The tomb of Xin Zhui, also known as "Lady Dai," is discovered in a hill in the Yangtse Valley, China. Her body is found in a remarkable state of preservation.

1972 Hunters find extremely well-preserved human corpses in Qilakitsoq, Greenland. The 500-year-old mummies include a six-month-old baby, a four-year-old boy, and six women of various ages.

1976 The embalmed body of Eva Perón is finally buried in Buenos Aires, Argentina. She has the best-preserved corpse in the world at this time.

1977 Rameses II becomes the first Egyptian pharaoh to visit Europe, when his mummy is taken to Paris for X-rays and other tests.

Workers in northeastern Russia dig up a 40,000-year-old baby woolly mammoth, which they nickname "Dima."

1978 Professor Gunther von Hagens invents plastination. In this process, human corpses are preserved by replacing all the fluids of the body with synthetic materials such as silicone rubber, epoxy resin, or polyester.

1984 The bodies of three sailors from Sir John Franklin's expedition are discovered in the Canadian Arctic. The icy conditions have preserved their bodies.

"Lindow Man" is discovered preserved in Lindow Moss bog in England. Although he has lain there for about 2,000 years, scientists are able to work out how Lindow Man died, how old he was, and what he ate for his last meal.

1991 German climbers find Ötzi the Iceman on top of a glacier near the Austro-Italian border.

1992 The face of Yde Girl is reconstructed by medical artist Richard Neave.

1993 A team of Russian archaeologists, led by Natalia Polosmak, uncover a 2,500-year-old tomb in the Altai Mountains in Russia. The tomb contains the bodies of six horses, and a woman preserved in a block of ice.

1994 English artist Damien Hirst preserves the body of a lamb in formaldehyde.

Dr. Bob Brier, a mummy researcher from the US, makes a modern mummy using ancient Egyptian procedures and tools. This is the first attempt in 2,000 years to treat a corpse using the methods that preserved the pharaohs of ancient Egypt.

1995 Anthropologist Dr. Johan Reinhard stumbles upon the body of a young girl, barely into her teens, on top of Mount Ampato in the Peruvian Andes. Nicknamed "Juanita," she is the best-preserved Inca mummy ever discovered.

1996 A group of Chachapoya mummies are discovered in a cache in the forest of the Peruvian Andes. Unfortunately, the looters who find the mummies damage some of them by cutting the cloth wrappings in search of jewelry.

The Valley of the Golden Mummies is discovered at Bahariya Oasis in Egypt. Later excavation work leads to the recovery of hundreds of the estimated 10,000 mummies that lie in the tombs. Some of the mummies retrieved are gilded from the head to the chest.

1997 In India, Mother Teresa of Calcutta dies. The nun's body is embalmed so that she can be displayed at her state funeral.

1999 Archaeologists find an enormous Inca cemetery in Puruchuco, Peru. More than 2,200 out of a possible 15,000 mummy bundles are unearthed.

Dr. Johan Reinhard finds a frozen boy, later known as "Llullaillaco Boy," along with two other preserved children, on Mount Llullaillaco in Argentina.

2004 A French team of archaeologists discover hundreds of mummies crammed into a maze of underground shafts and corridors in Saqqara, Egypt. Some of the mummies are wrapped in linen and encased in sealed coffins and stone sarcophagi.

EGYPTIAN DYNASTIES

Ancient Egypt's history is usually divided into 31 dynasties, a system devised by an Egyptian scholar called Manetho in the 3rd century AD. Historians revise the names and dates when new discoveries are made.

dynasties

EARLY DYNASTIC PERIOD

1st Dynasty c. 3100–2890 BC
Narmer 3100 BC
Djer 3000 BC
Djet 2980 BC
Den 2950 BC
Anedjib 2925 BC
Semerkhet 2900 BC
Qaa 2890 BC
2nd Dynasty c. 2890–2686 BC
Hetepsekhemwy 2890 BC
Raneb 2865 BC
Nynetjer
Weneg
Sened
Peribsen 2700 BC
Khasekhemwy 2686 BC

OLD KINGDOM

3rd Dynasty c. 2688–2613 BC
Sanakht 2686–2667 BC
Djoser 2667–2648 BC
Sekhemkhet 2648–2640 BC
Khaba 2640–2637 BC
Huni 2637–2613 BC
4th Dynasty c. 2613–2498 BC
Snefru 2613–2589 BC
Khufu* 2589–2566 BC
Radjedef 2566–2558 BC
Khafra 2558–2532 BC
Menkaura 2532–2503 BC
Shepseskaf 2503–2498 BC
also known as Cheops
5th Dynasty c. 2494–2345 BC
Userkaf 2494–2487 BC
Sahura 2487–2475 BC
Neferirkara 2475–2455 BC
Shepseskara 2455–2448 BC
Raneferef 2448–2445 BC
Nyuserra 2445–2421 BC
Menkauhor 2421–2414 BC
Djedkara 2414–2375 BC
Unas 2375–2345 BC
6th Dynasty c. 2345–2181 BC
Teti 2345–2323 BC
Userkara 2323–2321 BC
Pepy I 2321–2287 BC
Merenre 2287–2278 BC
Pepy II 2278–2184 BC
Nitocris (female) 2184–2181 BC

FIRST INTERMEDIATE PERIOD

7th–8th Dynasties 2181–2125 BC
This was an unstable period in Egypt's history, when there were many temporary kings.
9th–10th Dynasties c. 2160–2055 BC
Egypt ruled from Herakleopolis.
11th Dynasty c. 2125–2055 BC (Thebes only)
Intef I 2125–2112 BC
Intef II 2112–2063 BC
Intef III 2063–2055 BC

MIDDLE KINGDOM

11th Dynasty 2055–1985 BC (all Egypt)
Mentuhotep II 2055–2004 BC
Mentuhotep III 2004–1992 BC

Mentuhotep IV 1992–1985 BC
12th Dynasty 1985–1795 BC
Amenemhat I 1985–1955 BC
Senusret I* 1965–1920 BC
Amenemhat II 1922–1878 BC
Senusret II* 1880–1874 BC
Senusret III* 1874–1855 BC
Amenemhat III 1855–1808 BC
Amenemhat IV 1808–1799 BC
Sobekneferu (female) 1799–1795 BC
also known as Sesotris
13th Dynasty c. 1795–1725 BC
14th Dynasty c. 1750–1650 BC
A group of minor kings who probably ruled at the same time as the 13th Dynasty.

SECOND INTERMEDIATE PERIOD

15th Dynasty c. 1648–1540 BC
16th Dynasty c. 1650–1550 BC
17th Dynasty c. 1650–1550 BC

NEW KINGDOM

18th Dynasty c. 1550–1295 BC
Ahmose 1550–1525 BC
Amenhotep I* 1525–1504 BC
Thutmose I 1504–1492 BC
Thutmose II 1492–1479 BC
Thutmose III 1479–1425 BC
Hatshepsut (female) 1473–1458 BC
Amenhotep II* 1427–1400 BC
Thutmose IV 1400–1390 BC
Amenhotep III* 1390–1352 BC
Amenhotep IV** 1352–1336 BC
Smenkhkare (female) 1338–1336 BC
Tutankhamun 1336–1327 BC
Ay 1327–1323 BC
Horemheb 1323–1295 BC
also known as Amenophis
**often known as Akhenaten*
19th Dynasty c. 1295–1186 BC
Rameses I* 1295–1294 BC
Seti I 1294–1279 BC
Rameses II* 1279–1213 BC
Merenptah 1213–1203 BC
Amenmessul (female) 1203–1200 BC
Seti II 1200–1194 BC
Siptah 1194–1188 BC
Tauwosret (female) 1188–1186 BC
also spelled Ramses
20th Dynasty c. 1186–1069 BC
Sethakhte 1186–1184 BC
Rameses III* 1184–1153 BC
Rameses IV* 1153–1147 BC
Rameses V* 1147–1143 BC
Rameses VI* 1143–1136 BC
Rameses VII* 1136–1129 BC
Rameses VIII* 1129–1126 BC
Rameses IX* 1126–1108 BC
Rameses X* 1108–1099 BC
Rameses XI* 1099–1069 BC
also spelled Ramses

THIRD INTERMEDIATE PERIOD

21st Dynasty c. 1069–945 BC
Smendes 1069–1043 BC
Amenemnisu 1043–1039 BC
Psusennes I 1039–991 BC

Amenemope 993–984 BC
Osorkon I 984–978 BC
Siamun 978–959 BC
Psusennes II 959–945 BC
22nd Dynasty c. 945–715 BC
Sheshonq I 945–924 BC
Osorkon II 924–889 BC
Takelot I 899–874 BC
Sheshonq II c. 890 BC
Osorkon II 874–850 BC
Takelot II 850–825 BC
Sheshonq III 825–773 BC
Pimay 773–767 BC
Sheshonq IV 767–730 BC
Osorkon IV 730–715 BC
23rd Dynasty c. 818–715 BC
24th Dynasty c. 727–715 BC

LATE KINGDOM

25th Dynasty c. 747–656 BC
Piy 747–716 BC
Shabaqo 716–702 BC
Shabitqo 702–690 BC
Taharqa 690–664 BC
Tanutamani 664–656 BC
26th Dynasty 664–525 BC
Necho I 672–664 BC
Psamtek I 664–610 BC
Necho II 610–595 BC
Psamtek II 595–589 BC
Apries 589–570 BC
Ahmose II 570–526 BC
Psamtek III 526–525 BC
27th Dynasty c. 525–405 BC (1st Persian dynasty)
Cambyses 525–522 BC
Darius I 522–486 BC
Xerxes I 486–465 BC
Artaxerxes I 465–424 BC
Darius II 424–405 BC
28th Dynasty c. 404–399 BC
Amyrtaios 404–399 BC
29th Dynasty c. 399–380 BC
Nepherites I 399–393 BC
Psammuthis 393 BC
Hakoris 393–380 BC
Nepherites II 380 BC
30th Dynasty c. 380–343 BC
Nectanebo I 380–362 BC
Teos 362–360 BC
Nectanebo II 360–343 BC
31st Dynasty c. 343–332 BC (2nd Persian dynasty)
Ochus 343–338 BC
Arses 338–336 BC
Darius III Codomannus 336–332 BC

PTOLEMAIC PERIOD

First pharaoh:
Alexander the Great* of Macedon 333–323 BC
Macedonian conqueror of Egypt
Last pharaohs:
Ptolemy I* 305–285 BC
Cleopatra VII** (female) 51–30 BC
founder of the Ptolemaic dynasty
**last of the Ptolemaic rulers*
Egypt became part of the Roman empire in 30 BC, following the defeat of Cleopatra VII at the Battle of Actium.

GLOSSARY

Terms in italics are other glossary entries.

Afterlife Life after death.

Akh Ancient Egyptians believed this was the part of the spirit that existed forever. It went into the heavens and circled the stars.

Amulet Charm worn by the living or placed on a *mummy* to ward off evil spirits or bring good luck. Amulets often took the form of plants, animals, or parts of the human body.

Ancient Egypt Period in Egypt's history when the region was ruled by *pharaohs*.

Ankh Ancient Egyptian symbol of life, which was carried by the gods and by royalty.

Antechamber Small room in a *tomb* that leads to a larger, more important room.

Apis bull Sacred bull that ancient Egyptians believed to be the physical incarnation of the god Ptah. When the bull died, it was mummified and placed in a *tomb* called the Serapeum.

Archaeologist Scientist who studies human history through the excavation and analysis of human remains, buildings, and *artifacts*.

Artifact Human-made object that is often unearthed during archaeological digs.

Atef Crown with two large feathers on the top. It was one of the symbols of the Egyptian god Osiris.

Aztecs Native American civilization that ruled most of Mexico from the late 14th century AD until the early 16th century. The word Aztec means "someone who comes from Aztlán," an unknown location north of Mexico.

Ba In ancient Egyptian religion, this was one form of a person's spirit in the *afterlife*. It was represented by a bird with a human head.

Bacteria Single-celled microorganisms that live in and around us. Some cause dead bodies to decay.

Bog Wet, spongy expanse of decomposing vegetation. Dead bodies can be naturally mummified in some types of bogs. This is because bogs have high acid levels and low oxygen levels. The acidity and lack of oxygen limits the growth of bacteria that decay bodies.

Buchis bull Sacred bull that ancient Egyptians believed was the physical incarnation of the gods Osiris and Ra. It was also linked to the god of war, Montu.

Cache In *Egyptology*, a cache is a secret hiding place where royal *mummies* were concealed by priests after *tombs* had been looted by robbers.

Canopic jar Ancient Egyptian jar with a lid in the shape of a god's head. They were used to store *embalmed* internal organs.

Carbon dating Technique used to discover the age of an organic object, such as a dead body, by measuring the amount of Carbon 14 it contains. Also known as radiocarbon dating.

Cartouche Oval-shaped group of Egyptian *hieroglyphs*, in which the birth and coronation names of a *pharaoh* were inscribed. Its function was to magically protect the name of the king.

Catacomb Underground location for burials, with recesses for individual *tombs*.

Cryonics Chilling a recently deceased person to stop them from decomposing. Cryonics patients ask to be preserved in this way in the hope that medical science will one day develop techniques to revive them and cure any condition that may have killed them.

CT scan Computed tomography scan (also known as a CAT scan). A computerized X-ray procedure that produces cross-sectional images of the body. The images are far more detailed than X-ray films, and can reveal diseases or abnormalities in tissue and bone.

DNA Material inside the nucleus of cells that carries genetic information. The scientific name for DNA is deoxyribonucleic acid.

Dynasty Succession of rulers from the same family or line. *Egyptologists* usually divide *ancient Egypt's* history into 31 dynasties up to the arrival of Alexander the Great.

Egyptologist Historian or *archaeologist* who specializes in the study of *ancient Egypt* by examining its sites, *artifacts*, and documents.

Embalming Artificial preservation of a dead body from decay using chemicals, salts, perfumes, and ointments.

Formaldehyde Bacteria-killing substance discovered in 1868. It is used in *embalming* as a chemical preservative.

Hieroglyphs Realistic or stylized pictures of actual objects, animals, or human beings used by the ancient Egyptians to represent words, syllables, or sounds. This system of writing is known as hieroglyphics.

Incas Group of Quechuan peoples who established a great empire that stretched from northern Ecuador to central Chile. The capital was Cuzco, Peru. Their empire lasted from about AD 1100 until Spain conquered the region in the early 1530s.

Internal organs Separate parts of the body, such as the heart and the lungs, that perform a specific function to keep the body alive.

Ka Life-force that, according to the ancient Egyptians, entered each person's body at birth. It left the body upon the death of the person and received offerings of food that ensured the survival of the deceased in the *afterlife*.

Mastaba Arabic word for "bench." It has been used to describe early Egyptian *tombs* where the building above the ground was a rectangular structure with a flat roof, resembling a bench.

Mummiform Means "in the shape of a *mummy*." The term is often used when

describing the body-shaped coffins in which some ancient Egyptians were buried.

Mummy Dead body that has been preserved from decay, either naturally or artificially.

Mummy mask Mask that represents the real or idealized face of a dead person. It was placed over a *mummy's* face.

Natron Moisture-absorbing salt used in *ancient Egypt* to dry out a corpse before it was mummified. Natron occurs naturally and is found in dry lake beds.

Nemes Striped headcloth worn only by the Egyptian *pharaoh*.

Papyrus Water reed that was once abundant in Egypt. The ancient Egyptians processed papyrus into a form of paper, which was used for writing down important records.

Peat Brown organic matter similar to soil. It is formed from partly decomposed plants, especially sphagnum moss.

Pectoral Ornamental pendant worn on the chest. Pectorals were sometimes enclosed in an Egyptian *mummy's* bandages.

Pharaoh Title given to the rulers of *ancient Egypt*. The word means "great house," and originally referred to the royal palace rather than the king.

Pyramid Structure with a square base and triangular sides. In *ancient Egypt*, pyramids were built of stone or mud brick. They were mainly royal *tombs*, but some may have had other purposes.

Relic Part of the remains of a holy person, or some item connected with a dead holy person.

Sarcophagus Stone container that usually housed a coffin and body (or *mummy*). The surface of an ancient Egyptian sarcophagus was often inscribed with texts to assist the deceased in the journey through the *underworld*.

Scarab Egyptian dung-beetle, and also a gem carved to resemble one. The ancient Egyptians considered the dung-beetle lucky, and imagined their god Khepri as a scarab.

Shabti Miniature figures made in the image of servants, and buried with important people in *ancient Egypt*. They were supposed to perform manual work for the deceased in the *afterlife*.

Shrine Place of worship associated with some sacred object, person, or event.

Shroud Large sheet of fabric that is used to wrap a dead body.

Tomb Grave, monument, or building where the body of a dead person is laid.

Underworld Mythological place where the souls of the deceased are reputed to go.

Valley of the Kings Secluded valley west of the Nile River in Egypt where many *pharaohs* were buried in hidden *tombs*.

INDEX

ACKNOWLEDGMENTS

Dorling Kindersley would like to thank Alyson Lacewing for proofreading; Sue Lightfoot for the index; Christine Heilman for text Americanization.

Dorling Kindersley Ltd. is not responsible and does not accept liability for the availability or content of any website other than its own, or for any exposure to offensive, harmful, or inaccurate material that may appear on the Internet. Dorling Kindersley Ltd. will have no liability for any damage or loss caused by viruses that may be downloaded as a result of looking at and browsing the websites that it recommends. Dorling Kindersley downloadable images are the sole copyright of Dorling Kindersley Ltd., and may not be reproduced, stored, or transmitted in any form or by any means for any commercial or profit-related purpose without prior written permission of the copyright owner.

Picture Credits
The publisher would like to thank the following for their kind permission to reproduce their photographs:

Abbreviations key:
t-top, b-bottom, r-right, l-left, c-center, a-above, f-far

1 DK Images: Luxor Hotel's King Tut Museum c. 2 Corbis: Yann Arthus-Bertrand c. 3 Eurelios: c. 4–5 www.bridgeman.co.uk: Egyptian National Museum, Cairo, Egypt/Giraudon. 7 DK Images: Peter Hayman/British Museum br. 8 Corbis: Charles & Josette Lenars bl. 8 DK Images: British Museum ca, br. 8–9 NKA/Greenland National Museum. 9 Corbis: Charles & Josette Lenars tc; Chris Rainier bl. 9 Sandlin Associates Picture Library: tr. 10 Corbis: Newbury Jeffery bl. 10 Magnum: Bruno Barbey crb. 10 Science Photo Library: Prof's P. Motta & T. Naguro cfl. 11 Corbis: Baldev r. 11 Science Photo Library: Niedersachsisches Landes Museum, Germany/Munoz-Yague br. 12 Corbis: Giraud Philippe l; Richard T. Nowitz c. 12 DK Images: Alistair Duncan bc. 12–13 Corbis: Richard T. Nowitz. 13 DK Images: British Museum br; Peter Hayman/British Museum tr. 14 Alamy Images: Tor Eigeland bc. 14 Science Photo Library: John Sanford bl. 14–15 Corbis: Richard T. Nowitz. 15 DK Images: Alistair Duncan tr. 16 Corbis: Sandro Vannini l. 16 Topfoto.co.uk: The British Museum crb, bc. 17 www.bridgeman.co.uk: Egyptian National Museum, Cairo, Egypt cr; Giraudon tl. 17 Corbis: Carl & Ann Purcell bcl. 17 DK Images: Peter Hayman/The British Museum tr. 18 DK Images: Peter Hayman/The British Museum cb, cbl, cbr, l. 18 Jurgen Liepe: br. 18–19 Corbis: Craig Tuttle. 19 www.bridgeman.co.uk: cbl. 19 Corbis: Ludovic Maisant car. 19 DK Images: Peter Hayman/The British Museum cl; The British Museum br. 20 www.bridgeman.co.uk: cb, br; Lauros/Giraudon tl; Museo Archeologico Nazionale, Naples, Italy cr. 20 DK Images: Peter Hayman/British Museum bcl, bcr.

21 www.bridgeman.co.uk: cbl, tcl. 21 DK Images: Dave King/Pitt Rivers Museum, University of Oxford, Oxford cbr; Peter Hayman/The British Museum bc, cal, car. 21 Pelizaeus Museum, Hildesheim: r. 22 www.bridgeman.co.uk: Egyptian National Museum, Cairo, Egypt/Giraudon l. 22 Robert Harding Picture Library: cfr. 22–23 DK Images: Peter Hayman/The British Museum. 23 akg-images: br. 23 DK Images: Peter Hayman/The British Museum tl, tr, c, cr, cr, cfr. 24 Ancient Art & Architecture Collection: cfl. 24 DK Images: Peter Hayman/The British Museum cbl; 24-25 DK Images: The British Museum. 24–25 Jaques Livet. 25 Ancient Art & Architecture Collection: cra. 25 Corbis: Gian Berto Vanni br. 25 DK Images: Peter Hayman/The British Museum cla; The British Museum ca. 26 www.bridgeman.co.uk: Louvre, Paris, France, car. 26 DK Images: Peter Hayman/The British Museum l; The British Museum cbr. 27 Corbis: Gianni Dagli Orti cbl; Jonathan Blair r. 27 Corbis: tc. 28 Corbis: Carl & Ann Purcell c; Charles & Josette Lenars bcr; Peter Johnson tl. 29 Ancient Art & Architecture Collection: cla. 29 DK Images: Peter Hayman/The British Museum tl, bl, bcl, r; The British Museum c.

30 www.bridgeman.co.uk: Brooklyn Museum of Art, New York, USA cfl. 30 Corbis: Sandro Vannini bc. 30 The Art Archive: Musée du Louvre Paris/Dagli Orti cb. 30–31 Ancient Art & Architecture Collection. 30–31 Corbis: Roger Wood. 31 The Art Archive: Musée du Louvre Paris/Dagli Orti tr. 31 Topfoto.co.uk: The British Museum bc. 32 www.bridgeman.co.uk: Bibliotheque Nationale, Paris, France, Giraudon c. 32 DK Images: The British Museum r. 32 Musee de Louvre: clb. 33 Corbis: Araldo de Luca r; Vanni Archive bcr. 33 DK Images: Peter Hayman/The British Museum tl, cbl; The British Museum clb, tcl. 34 DK Images: Alistair Duncan tl; Peter Hayman/The British Museum clb, bl, cbl. 34–35 Corbis: Gianni Dagli Orti. 35 The Ancient Egypt Picture Library: r. 35 www.bridgeman.co.uk: Louvre, Paris, France, tl. 35 Werner Forman Archive: The Egyptian Museum, Cairo cal. 36 The Ancient Egypt Picture Library: cr, cfl. 36 Corbis: Archivo Iconografico, S.A. cl. 36 The Art Archive: Egyptian Museum Cairo/Dagli Orti tl. 36 Robert Harding Picture Library: K.Gillham bl. 37 The Ancient Egypt Picture Library: cr, cfl. 37 Corbis: Archivo Iconografico, S.A. clb; Gianni Dagli Orti tl; Mike McQueen tr; Richard T. Nowitz crb. 38 Corbis: Hulton-Deutsch Collection tl. 38 Topfoto.co.uk: FotoWare bl. 38–39 popperfoto.com. 39 www.bridgeman.co.uk: The Stapleton Collection cra. 39 Corbis: Bettmann tr. 39 Mary Evans Picture Library: cra. 40 Corbis: Hulton-Deutsch Collection cfl. 40–41 www.bridgeman.co.uk: The Stapleton Collection. 41 www.bridgeman.co.uk: Egyptian National Museum, Cairo, Egypt tr. 41 Griffith Institute, Oxford: crb. 42 Ancient Art & Architecture Collection: cra. 42 Corbis: Archivo Iconografico, S.A. bl; Roger Wood tl. 42–43 akg-images: Egyptian Museum, Cairo.

42–43 DK Images: Luxor Hotel's King Tut Museum. 43 Corbis: Sandro Vannini tr. 43 Corbis: br. 44 www.bridgeman.co.uk: Archives Charmet c. 44 DK Images: Peter Hayman/The British Museum br; The British Museum bcl. 44 The Art Archive: Malmaison Musée du Chateau/Dagli Orti cfl. 44 Royal Pharmaceutical Society of Great Britain: tr. 45 DK Images: Judith Miller/Marie Antiques tcl. 45 Ronald Grant Archive: cl. 45 Peery's Egyptian Theater: car. 45 Topfoto.co.uk: bc. 46 DK Images: Geoff Brightling l. 46 Science Photo Library: Alexander Tsiaras cr, br. 47 Science Photo Library: Klaus Guldbrandsen tcr; NIBSC tr; Peter Menzel tl; Volker Steger tcl. 47 The University of Manchester: b. 48 Ancient Art & Architecture Collection: c. 48 www.bridgeman.co.uk: Museum of Fine Arts, Boston, Massachusetts, USA, Gift of the Egypt Exploration Fund cfr. 48 Corbis: Bettmann br. 48 DK Images: Andrew Butler bcl. 48 Science Photo Library: Mark A. Schneider br. 49 Eurelios: r. 49 Science Photo Library: James King-Holmes cal, cbl. 50 South American Pictures: t. 50–51 Eurelios. 51 Eurelios: tr, cla, c, crb. 52 Corbis: Gianni Dagli Orti cfl. 52 Werner Forman Archive: bl. 52–53 South American Pictures. 53 Corbis: Engel Bros. Media Inc. tr. 53 Eurelios: crb. 53 South American Pictures: tl. 54 DK Images: Michael Dunning tl, br. 54 South American Pictures: cb. 54 Museum Fur Volkerkunde Berlin: bcl. 55 The Art Archive: Biblioteca Nazionale Marciana Venice/Dagli Orti tr. 55 Eurelios: l. 55 National Geographic Image Collection: car. 55 Corbis: b. 56 Corbis: Hubert Stadler t. 56 Michael Holford: bl. 56 Johan Reinhard: br, bcr. 57 Associated Press: Martin Mejia b. 57 Johan Reinhard: tr, cfl. 58 Corbis: Bettmann crb, cbr; Galen Rowell l. 58 Queen West Gallery District: Lewis Cottlow bc; William R. Jamieson cl. 58 South American Pictures: cfr. 59 Corbis: Hulton-Deutsch Collection cbl. 59 South American Pictures: br. 59 Getty Images: Stone cfl. 60 Bryan And Cherry Alexander Photography: b. 60 www.bridgeman.co.uk: Hudson Bay Company, Canada cr. 60 National Portrait Gallery, London: tr. 61 Owen Beattie: r. 61 Corbis: Ralph White bl. 61 Mary Evans Picture Library: cl. 61 National Maritime Museum, London: cfl. 62 Corbis: Marc Garanger l. 62 South Tyrol Museum Of Archaeology: crb, bcl, cbr. 63 South Tyrol Museum Of Archaeology: tr, clb, bl, br, cal, cfl. 64 Science Photo Library: Silkborg Museum, Denmark/Munoz-Yague tl; Silkeborg Museum, Denmark/Munoz-Yague clb. 64-65 Robert Harding Picture Library: R.Ashworth. 65 DK Images: Flag Fen Excavations br; Geoff Dann, The British Museum bcr; University of Archaeology & Anthropology of Cambridge br. 65 Silkeborg Museum, Denmark: tc. 66 DK Images: Museum of London car; The British Museum cl, br. 67 DK Images: National Museum of Copenhagen c. 67 Science Photo Library: Archaeologisches Landesmuseum, Germany/Munoz-Yague crb; Drents Museum,

Holland/Munoz-Yague tc, tcl, tcr. 67 National Museum Of Wales: tr. 68 www.bridgeman.co.uk: clb. 68 Fortean Picture Library: Dr Elmar R. Gruber tl. 68 Magnum: Bruno Barbey br. 69 www.bridgeman.co.uk: Lauros/Giraudon br. 69 Corbis: Chris Lisle bc; Galen Rowell cl. 69 Fortean Picture Library: Andreas Trottmann t. 69 Getty Images: cfl. 70 Impact Photos: tcr. 70–71 Corbis: Yann Arthus-Bertrand tr. 71 Impact Photos: tc. 72 Corbis: Yann Arthus-Bertrand clb, bl. 72 Impact Photos: tr, cla, cfl. 72–73 Corbis: Alinari Archives. 73 www.bridgeman.co.uk: Galleria degli Uffizi, Florence, Italy tl. 73 Corbis: Yann Arthus-Bertrand r. 74 Corbis: Staffan Widstrand cl. 74 DK Images: Dave King/Courtesy of the National Museum of Wales tr, cl. 75 Corbis: Jonathan Blair tr; Reuters br. 75 Jean Plassard: tl. 75 Science Photo Library: Novosti cla; Philippe Plailly/Eurelios cfl. 76 Corbis: Charles O'Rear, cbr; Setboun l. 76–77 Corbis: Charles O'Rear. 76–77 Novosti (London). 77 Novosti (London): tr, cra, cb, cfr. 78 Novosti (London): bc. 78 Science Photo Library: Philippe Plailly/Eurelios cl. 79 Ancient Art & Architecture Collection: tl. 79 www.bridgeman.co.uk: Hermitage, St. Petersburg, Russia cla. 79 Corbis: Earl & Nazima Kowall br. 79 Novosti (London): tr. 80 Corbis: Newbury Jeffery r; Reza; Webistan l. 81 Corbis: Dean Conger cr; Newbury Jeffery cfr, l; Reza; Webistan tc, bcr, cbr. 82 Corbis: Keren Su t. 82 Dennis Cox/ChinaStock: Wang Lu c. 82–83 Corbis: Asian Art & Archaeology, Inc. 83 Dennis Cox/ChinaStock: cbr; Wang Lu ca. 84 Sandlin Associates Picture Library: cb. 85 Sandlin Associates Picture Library: tr, br, bcl, bcr, cfl, cfr, tcl. 86 Corbis: bl; Reuters ca. 86 Pa Photos: cbr. 87 Alcor Life Extension Foundation: cr, clb, tcl. 87 Associated press: tcr. 87 Corbis: Michael Macor/San Francisco Chronicle tr. 87 Kobal Collection: Warner Bros br. 87 Topfoto.co.uk: tl. 88 White Cube Gallery: Damien Hirst bc. 88 Powerstock: t. 88 Royal College of Surgeons: Museum of Royal College of Surgeons crb. 89 Gunther von Hagens, Institute for Plastination, Heidelberg, Germany (www.bodyworlds.com): tl, tr, br. 89 Library Services, University College London: bcl. 90–91 DK Images: Peter Anderson/Courtesy of The Bolton Metro Museum.

Jacket Images *Front:* Corbis: Bojan Brecelj (cl), Chris Rainier (cfl) Sandro Vannini (cfr); Science Photo Library: Niedersachsisches Landesmuseum, Germany/Munoz-Yague (cr). *Spine:* Getty/Photodisc Green. *Back:* Corbis: Charles O'Rear (cl), Gianni Dagli Orti (cfl), Nathan Benn (cfr). DK Images: Bolton Metro Museum (cr).

All other images © Dorling Kindersley.
For further information, see:
www.dkimages.com